Fight the Law and Win

What You Need to Know if You Are a Criminal Defendant or Care About Someone Who Is

Greg Hagopian
Criminal Defense Attorney
California Bar Association Certified
Specialist in Criminal Law

Disclaimers/Terms of Use

By consulting this guidebook all users understand, acknowledge, and agree to all of the following Disclaimers and Terms of Use.

This publication is for informational purposes only. None of the general legal topics discussed in this publication are to be construed as legal advice and should not be regarded as such. This book is not designed to replace any legal advice by Licensed and Qualified Legal Advisors.

This is an educational publication designed to educate users about legal topics and issues that impact individuals in general. These issues may or may not affect any individuals and if so, may affect individuals differently. The topics discussed in this publication are provided to facilitate your educated and informed discussions with your trusted legal advisor.

The information contained in this publication is believed to be accurate. However, laws, circumstances, and several other unknown factors can render any content contained herein to be unreliable, unusable, and/or inaccurate at any time and without notification. All users assume full responsibility for outcomes and results from application of or reliance on this material. All users accept full responsibility for consulting qualified legal counsel to discuss this material and their own unique legal concerns, issues, and circumstances. The author, publisher, and any affiliates make no offers, promises, warranties, or guarantees of any type to anyone by allowing access to this publication.

The Law Office of
Gregory Hagopian
115 South Church Street
Visalia, CA 93291
Phone: 559-302-9507
www.hagopianlawoffice.com

Table of Contents

Introduction

My name is Greg Hagopian, and I love the law. I love the criminal courts and, indeed, the entire judicial system. I remember wanting to be a lawyer when I was a 12-year-old kid arguing with my teachers. I was a competitive debater in school and studied American Government before going straight to law school. I not only took the California Bar Exam and passed on the first try, but I've become one of a handful of California Bar Association Certified Specialists in Criminal Law. This stuff excites me!

I understand that *you*, the person reading this book, very likely don't feel that way about the law right now. That's okay. Most people don't spend a lot of time in their daily lives thinking about the law. When you are charged with a crime, however, "the law" and the criminal justice system that implements the law become very real, very fast, and the process can be very scary.

I decided to write this book to answer what I know, from years of experience, are some of the questions that you have right now about what has happened to you, what is going to happen next, and what might happen in the future.

I cannot make a lawyer out of you. What I can do is give you some information about the process you are about to be put through, as a whole, and dispel some of the more harmful myths about the process.

So if you don't love the law like I love the law, again, that's okay. That's what people like me exist for. Hopefully, after reading this book you will, at the very least, feel a little more prepared and know a bit more about what to expect when you go to court.

If you need more help, you can always call my firm, the Law Office of Greg Hagopian, and someone will talk to you about coming on as one of our clients. We're here to help.

I have tried to keep my natural lawyerly verbosity to a minimum so that you can get through the entirety of this book in a manageable amount of time. Each chapter title clearly outlines the critical topics discussed in that chapter. Ideally, my suggestion would be to read this book, take notes in the blank "NOTE" pages at the end, and then take this book with you when you do finally consult with a lawyer, whether it be at the Law Office of Greg Hagopian or anywhere else.

Throughout this book, I will describe some of the different people who will affect your case. The following image identifies where some of these parties can be found in a court setting.

Good luck to you. With a little help and a little luck, you may one day be able to say, *"I fought the law, and I won."*

Chapter 1

What Just Happened?

It's a regular day at my office. A man and a woman in their fifties come in, looking very worried. Neither of them is the defendant. These are the parents. Their child is being accused of some kind of crime. He was arrested a few days ago and is being held in custody at the county jail. These people don't know what happened. They hope their child is innocent, though they honestly don't know. They've come to speak to a lawyer because that's what people do. They're wary. They know that lawyers are expensive, and they've heard that lawyers don't always have the best reputation for honesty. They never thought they would need a criminal defense lawyer. But here they are. They walk into the lion's den because that's what people do when they need a lawyer to help their child.

The very first question they are going to ask is almost always the same. It isn't how much I charge. It isn't what kind of defenses might exist. The question that has been burning up these parents since they heard of their child's arrest is . . . what's the worst-case scenario?

What can happen if I am convicted?

This is the first question that hits most people. It's terrifying. I'll try to make it a little easier to understand the sentencing scheme used in the courts in the state of California, and hopefully that will help you feel like you have a little better grasp of what's happening.

Chapter 2

Understanding the Charges and Sentencing Ranges

Felonies, Misdemeanors, and Infractions:

California categorizes its laws into Felonies, Misdemeanors, and Infractions.

Infractions are those things for which a person cannot be put in jail. Littering is an infraction. Speeding is an infraction. Infractions are violations of legal rules that are so small that most people don't even consider them "criminal acts." The penalty for being convicted of committing an infraction is usually just a fine.

A **misdemeanor** is a crime for which a person can be placed in the county jail for up to a year (some misdemeanors have a maximum sentence of only 6 months or even less). Most DUI cases are misdemeanors. Petty theft, simple assault, and possession of narcotics are all misdemeanors.

A **felony** is a crime for which a person can be placed in either the county jail or the state prison, for more than a year. Very serious felonies can result in life imprisonment or even the death penalty. Murder, rape, arson, robbery, and possession of narcotics for sale are all felonies. A theft or fraud may be a felony if enough money is involved. A DUI may be a felony if the defendant has 3 or more prior convictions within a 10-year period or if someone was injured due to the defendant's driving under the influence.

Sentencing Range:

In misdemeanor cases, the sentencing range will be a term of days (0–180 for example) that the judge may impose. In addition to the jail sentence, the court may place the person on probation for up to 5 years (more on probation in another chapter).

In felony cases, sentencing is a bit more complicated. Felony sentencing ranges have a low, middle, or high term (called a sentencing triad) that the court must choose from (for example, 16 months, 2 years, or 3 years for most felonies). A judge, however, in many cases may ignore the sentencing triad and place the defendant on felony probation. The court may then order the defendant to serve a term of between 0 and 365 days in the county jail as a term of that probation.[1] If the defendant violates probation, the court may then impose one of the triad sentences at a probation revocation hearing.

While it is impossible to list the possible sentences for every crime in a book of this size, below is the abbreviated sentencing range for the most common crimes a person can be accused of committing. I have not included the fines and fees that could be ordered. These fines vary by crime, by county, and whether or not restitution is ordered.

- First Time Driving Under the Influence — 2 to 180 days.
- Second Time Driving Under the Influence — 10 days to 1 year.
- Third Time Driving Under the Influence — 120 days to 1 year.
- Fourth Time Driving Under the Influence (or DUI Resulting in Injury) — 16 months, 2 years, or 3 years.
- Misdemeanor Battery — 0 to 180 days.
- Felony Assault[2] — 16 months, 2 years, or 3 years.

---

[1] In some cases, these sentences may be served outside of the county jail through work-release or house arrest.

[2] It may be beneficial at this point to pause for a moment to explain the difference between an "assault" and a "battery." A battery is any harmful or offensive touching that is purposefully done. An assault is an attempted battery. All batteries must include assaults (it is what lawyers call a "lesser included offense." All battery charges in California are misdemeanors. Once a battery becomes a felony we switch terminology to refer to felony

- Disturbing the Peace—0 to 90 days.
- Resisting, Obstructing, or Delaying a Peace Officer in the Performance of Their Duties—0 to 365 days.
- Petty Theft—0 to 180 days.
- Grand Theft—16 months, 2 years, or 3 years.
- Robbery—2 years, 3 years, or 5 years.
- Lewd Conduct with a Child Between 14-15 years old—16 months, 2 years, or 3 years.
- Lewd Conduct with a Child Under 14—3, 6, or 8 years.
- Statutory Rape—6 Months, 2 years, or 3 years.
- Forcible Rape—9 years, 11 years, or 13 years.
- Arson of a Residence—3 years, 5 years, or 8 years.
- Possession of a Firearm by a Felon—16 months, 2 years, or 3 years.
- Possession of an Assault Weapon—16 months, 2 years, or 3 years.
- Attempted Murder—7 years to life.
- Murder—25 years to life.

Felony Sentencing:

If a person is convicted of committing a felony, there are a number of things that can affect the sentence:

- What is the sentencing range for the crime charged?
- Is the defendant eligible and suitable for probation?
- Are there any "special allegations" charged?

---

assault. This may be an assault with force likely to produce great bodily injury, an assault with a deadly weapon, or an assault on a peace officer, etc. A felony assault does not require that anyone ever actually be touched, only that an attempt to do so was made under one of the felony conditions (with a deadly weapon, etc.). If a touching actually does take place, it may lead to the addition of what are called "special allegations." Which we'll discuss later.

Chapter 3

Understanding Special Allegations

SPECIAL ALLEGATIONS:

Oftentimes, more important than the "base term[3]" a "special allegation" charges that the defendant not only committed a crime, but either committed it in a certain way or committed it after having committed other crimes in the past.

Some crimes are called "priorable offenses." A priorable offense is one where after a first conviction any subsequent conviction carries a greater sentence. Driving Under the Influence is a "priorable offense." Petty theft is also a priorable offense. Possession of narcotics for sale is a priorable offense. Because the fact of a prior conviction affects the sentence, it must be charged and proved by the Prosecution.

Other special allegations include causing great bodily injury to a victim during the commission of a crime (3 additional years), committing a crime while out on bail (2 additional years), having a "prison prior" (1 additional year for each prior), and using a non-firearm deadly weapon (usually 1 additional year).

The two largest and most severe special allegations involve gangs and guns. The use of a firearm, even if done by a co-defendant, can add

---

[3] Meaning the sentence without any special allegations, including strike enhancements.

anywhere from 1 year (for simply being armed with a firearm) to 3 years (for simply being armed with an assault weapon) to 10 years for showing a gun during the commission of some felonies, to 20 years for discharging a firearm during the commission of a strike offense, to an ADDITIONAL (added to the base term) 25 years to life sentence for causing great bodily injury or death with a firearm during the commission of a strike offense.

Meanwhile, the commission of a felony crime for the benefit of a criminal street gang can increase a sentence anywhere from a few months (by making a misdemeanor into a felony) to 5 years for some felonies, 10 years for others, and 15 to life for some of the most serious. For example, carjacking is only a life crime when committed for the benefit of a criminal street gang. Extortion and witness intimidation go from being crimes carrying sentences of 3 or 4 years to carrying a sentence of 7 years to life when a gang enhancement is attached.

STRIKES:

A word about strike offenses:
Some particularly serious felonies were singled out several years ago as what are called "strike offenses" in the state of California.

The history of the three-strikes law in the state of California:

Like most of the United States, California saw an increase in crime starting in the early 1980s and peaking in the early 1990s. This increase, in some areas, amounted to as much as a doubling of the number of reported crimes during those years. The media, using emerging technologies including cable television and eventually Internet news outlets, magnified this problem in the eyes of the public by running almost constant stories about violent crime and criminals.

There is an old saying in the news business: "If it bleeds, it leads." And during the 1990s, stories about violent crime led almost every major news outlet, every day. The public's fear of their own house being robbed or of being held up at gunpoint in a parking lot surged. Eventually politicians began to feed on that fear by offering "get tough on crime" laws to make themselves appear to be the saviors of the population. All over the United States, such laws, including the three-strikes law in California, as well as the extremely harsh California Gang Enhancement legislation (as noted in Chapter 2), were passed.

The basic rules of the original three-strikes law were simple. There was a list of crimes that were considered to be either "serious" or "violent" felonies. If a crime was considered to be a "serious or violent" felony, then it was considered to be a "strike offense." A person who had one "strike prior" on their record (meaning a prior conviction for a strike offense), who was convicted of ANY other felony, would be ineligible for probation and would have the sentence for that felony doubled. A person who had two or more "strike priors" on their record and was convicted of ANY other felony would be sentenced to a MINIMUM of 25 years to life in the state prison.

Almost immediately the three-strikes law started to result in brutal and heartless sentences for minor offenses. When California passed the three-strikes law, it had decided to trust the various district attorneys' offices in the State to only request Three Strikes Sentencing in appropriate cases where the defendant was genuinely a continuing, violent menace to society. What California residents soon found out is that they should NEVER place that kind of trust in the hands of law enforcement, especially district attorneys who have to run for an elected office.

Cases showing the abuse of the three-strikes law:

In 1995, Curtis Wilkerson was sentenced to 25 years to life for shoplifting a pair of socks in a mall. His girlfriend was getting her hair done at the mall, and he was bored. The socks were worth $2.50. Mr. Wilkerson had two priors, both more than ten years old, for residential burglary. No one was home on either occasion, and Mr. Wilkerson served only as a lookout, never even entering the home on one of those occasions.

There is also the case of Lester Wallace, who was sentenced to 25 years to life for attempting to steal a car radio. The police caught him in the car. Mr. Wallace also had two prior convictions for non-violent residential burglaries. Lester Wallace was a schizophrenic whose case garnered some media attention when it was learned that he was abused by other inmates while incarcerated because of his mental condition.

In 1996, Shane Taylor was one of the MANY inmates sentenced to 25 years to life for personal possession (not possession for sale) of methamphetamine. His prior two offenses had both been committed in the same week 8 years prior and, again, consisted of him breaking into houses. In one house, Mr. Wallace stole nothing, and in the other he stole a checkbook with which he bought a pizza. (These cases and several others are discussed in the April 11, 2013, issue of *Rolling Stone*.)

Seeing these obvious abuses by prosecutors, in 2012 California voters approved an amendment to the three-strikes law over a massive campaign of objections by the very law enforcement whose heartless and gutless actions had made the amendment necessary.

Today in the state of California, anyone with one strike prior who is convicted of another felony is still ineligible for probation and can still expect to have the sentence for that felony doubled. However, a person with two or more strike priors only becomes eligible to be sentenced to 25 years to life if they are convicted of another serious or violent felony.

All is not necessarily lost, however, for defendants with strike priors. It is also possible for the sentencing judge to "strike a strike." This means that the court can choose to ignore a strike prior for sentencing purposes if they believe that it will serve the interests of justice. Any competent lawyer will make a motion (request) to the judge to have them consider this if their client has a strike prior. This is referred to as a Romero Motion (named for the defendant whose lawyer fought all the way to the California Supreme Court to secure the right of the trial judge to exercise this type of discretion).

SO HOW MUCH TIME AM I LOOKING AT?

Felony sentencing in California is sometimes a maddening game of numbers. Let us take the hypothetical case of Adam, who is a Crip gang member. Adam has a prior conviction for selling drugs for the benefit of the Crip criminal street gang. Let's say that Adam is walking around the neighborhood with a concealed firearm one day, and he finds a spot that he thinks is good for graffiti. Adam spray-paints "Crips" on the wall.

Using standard California felony sentencing, we start with the fact that Adam is guilty of being a felon in possession of a firearm, of which the maximum term is 3 years. He is also guilty of illegally carrying a concealed firearm. This crime by itself would carry a maximum term of 3 years, but since there is already another felony offense, California adds only "1/3 the midterm" of any secondary offense (usually), meaning that 8 months is added for this offense.

Adam has also committed a felony vandalism. Let us assume the damage was more than $400, making it a felony. Felony vandalism will also add 8 months to this sentence. We now have a term of 4 years and 4 months . . . but we aren't done yet. Adam has a strike prior (any felony, even possession for sale of narcotics, when committed for the benefit of a street gang is a strike), and a person with a strike prior gets any future felony sentence doubled. So, Adam is now facing 8 years and 8 months . . . but we aren't done yet.

Adam committed the vandalism while armed with a firearm, which in this case adds a year to his sentence. We are now at 9 years and 8 months . . . but we aren't done yet. Adam committed this crime to benefit a criminal street gang (the Crips). The commission of this type of felony for the benefit of a criminal street gang adds up to 4 years to the sentence. We therefore find ourselves in the position where Adam is facing a prison term of **13 YEARS AND 4 MONTHS** for spray-painting a wall . . . but we aren't done yet.

You see, normally Adam would be able to earn what are called "half-time" credits. Meaning that if he doesn't cause any problems and agrees to work, helping around the prison, he will be released after half of his sentence is served. Unfortunately for Adam, because he has a strike prior, he is required to serve out two-thirds of any sentence. That means Adam will be eligible for parole . . . in a little less than 9 years.

Except we aren't done yet. As it turns out, in 2016, Proposition 57 was passed. Under Proposition 57, because Adam was not sentenced for any "violent felony," we ignore all of the special enhancements and the consecutive sentences for additional crimes. Adam must serve out the sentence for the "primary felony" and then he will be eligible for parole. Any of the felonies in this hypothetical could be the "primary offense" because they all carry the same sentence. Since the length of the sentence is calculated "excluding the imposition of an enhancement, consecutive sentence, or alternative sentence," we ignore the strike prior, we ignore the gun enhancement, we ignore the other two felonies, and Adam, who is now eligible for half-time credits, is eligible for parole (assuming he causes no problems and agrees to help around the prison) in 18 months (one half of 3 years).

SAY WHAT?

I very much wish that I could make criminal sentencing easier to understand. The fact is, however, that a system designed to punish a dizzying array of different types of offenses in a way that attaches some kind of increasing and decreasing severity of punishments to match increasing and decreasing severity of offenses . . . is going to be extremely complicated. The state of California often seems to have gone out of its way to make it unnecessarily MORE SO.

What you will want to know in YOUR CASE, however, is:

- What is the base term minimum and maximum;
- What special allegations are charged, and how do they affect the sentence;
- And finally, what kind of credits will you be getting if convicted?

Chapter 4

Understanding Custody Assignments

WHERE WILL I SERVE OUT MY CUSTODY SENTENCE?

A few years ago, this was a fairly complicated question to answer. Since 2011, however, it has become . . . more complicated. To explain, it might be best to start with the pre-2011 world.

Pre-2011, anyone convicted of a misdemeanor and sentenced to jail time was placed in the county jail (maybe) to serve their sentence. This is also where everyone who is awaiting trial and cannot make bail[4] is held. A person who was convicted of a felony and placed on probation would also typically serve out a sentence of between 0 and 360 days in the county jail (maybe), as a term of their probation.

I say "maybe" in the county jail because most counties have ways that many defendants who are either convicted of misdemeanors or placed on felony probation can serve their sentences outside of a jail cell. This includes house arrest and being placed on a sheriff's work program, where the defendant would work for the sheriff's department doing "community service" type jobs during the day but going home at night.

---

[4] We will discuss bail in detail in a later chapter.

Back then, everyone who received a felony non-probation sentence (all of which are more than a year) would go to the state prison.

Since 2011, there are now a number of felonies for which a person serves out a felony non-probation sentence in the county jail. This book cannot list all of the offenses that either are or are not served out "locally," but suffice it to say that they are mostly the less serious felony crimes.

LET'S ASSUME I'M GOING TO PRISON; TELL ME ABOUT THE CALIFORNIA DEPARTMENT OF CORRECTIONS

There are 35 different California state prisons. They are split up both by gender (male prisons and female prisons) and security ranking (from Low Security (Level 1) to Maximum Security (Level 4), to Special Housing Units, to Death Row.

A few "standout" prisons:

Pelican Bay:

California's only "supermax" prison is Pelican Bay State Prison. Pelican Bay is home to the "SHU" or Special Housing Unit. This is the highest security wing in any prison in California. Typically, the inhabitants of the "SHU" are gang leaders, violent psychopaths, or any other persons the California Department of Corrections has determined need to be kept in permanent solitary confinement under high security.

San Quentin:

San Quentin is home to California's Death Row.

Folsom:

Made famous by Johnny Cash and often thought of as a place full of really scary people, in reality Folsom Prison is a minimum to medium security prison.

Corcoran:

Home to Sirhan Sirhan, Charles Manson (before he died), and at one time, the police officers from the Rampart Gang Fiasco (convicted of planting

14

evidence, etc.) Corcoran is a maximum-security facility that has housed some of the big names in crime.

Mule Creek:

As of 2005, Mule Creek became California's only prison made up entirely of protective custody wings (sometimes called "special-needs yards"). Mule Creek is currently home to the Menendez brothers.

Out of State:

California's prison system is massively overcrowded. To help solve this problem, the state of California has contracted with other states, and inmates are now increasingly being sent to out-of-state prisons. This usually happens in cases of long-term prison commitments (more than 10 years).

How is it decided where I will go?

Every new prisoner starts out spending several days to several months being "classified." During this period, the California Department of Corrections (CDC) decides where the prisoner should be kept for the duration of their sentence.

The CDC considers a number of factors including:

- What crime or crimes was the defendant convicted of? The more violent, the higher the security area the defendant is likely to be put in.
- Is the defendant at risk and in need of protective custody? This may be based on the crime (all child molesters, for instance, are placed into protective custody) or other factors (the defendant is a snitch or a former police officer, etc.)
- Is the defendant a gang member? Gang members are assumed to be trouble and are placed into higher security prisons.

NOTE: If a prisoner was convicted of the special allegation that a crime was committed "for the benefit of a criminal street gang" (see Chapter 3 – "Special Allegations"), they will certainly be classified as a gang member. If the prisoner has obvious prison tattoos, they will also certainly be classified as a gang member. Otherwise it depends largely on the answers they give during their classification interviews.

FURTHER NOTE: The California Department of Corrections (CDC) does not consider gang membership to be permanent. Gang members may, and are encouraged to, "drop out" of their gangs. In order to do this, however, the CDC requires dropouts to "debrief." The debrief is an interview done with law enforcement officers where the dropout is asked to give the officers information about their former gang life and associates in exchange for being allowed to be moved into protective custody.

THAT ALL SOUNDS TERRIBLE!
IS THERE ANY WAY TO GET A CRIMINAL CASE DISMISSED?

Chapter 5

How to Get a Criminal Case Dismissed

IS THERE ANY WAY TO GET A CRIMINAL CASE DISMISSED?

There are several ways to get a criminal case dismissed. A case can be dismissed either by the prosecutor or the judge.

How and why do judges dismiss cases?

There are a small number of times when a Superior Court judge may dismiss a criminal case. What is much more common is that the judge will rule that certain evidence that the prosecutor would need in order to convince a jury to convict the defendant cannot be shown to the jury. The legal term for such evidence is "suppressed evidence."

When can a judge outright dismiss a case?

1. **The Demur:**
A "demur" is a challenge to the government's ability to bring the criminal case at all. The defense attorney brings a proper "demur" to the case when they show that the charged offense is not really illegal, the law is unconstitutional, the crime took place outside the geographical jurisdiction of the court, or the statute of limitations had run out before charges were brought.

2. The Preliminary Hearing:

In felony cases, the prosecutor is required, prior to trial, to put on a Preliminary Hearing. To put on a Preliminary Hearing means to call witnesses and present evidence, showing the judge that there is enough evidence that the defendant probably committed the charged crimes. If the judge does not feel that the prosecutor has met this burden, the judge may dismiss the case without the need for a trial.

3. The 1118 Motion:

At trial, if the prosecution puts on so little evidence or evidence of such poor quality that no reasonable jury could find the defendant guilty beyond a reasonable doubt, the defense attorney should bring an 1118 Motion (named for California Penal Code Section 1118), and the judge may dismiss the case without asking the jury to make a decision.

4. The Serna/Doggett Motion:

Occasionally, criminal charges are brought without the defendant knowing about it until months or years later. In these cases, even though the prosecutor has brought criminal charges within the statute of limitations, the defendant may ask that the case be dismissed because it is unfair to ask them to defend themselves against charges of violating the law so long ago.

5. The Trombetta-Youngblood Motion:

This motion argues that when law enforcement either intentionally or due to extreme negligence destroys evidence that the defendant would need in order to defend himself, any trial would be unfair and the judge is allowed to dismiss the case.

When can a judge suppress evidence?

1. The Miranda Motion:

Named for the Supreme Court case of <u>Miranda v. Arizona</u>, which declared that the police needed to inform people of their rights before custodial interrogation.

What that means is that before the police can detain a person and interrogate them for information, the police are required to read that person their "**Miranda Rights**." These rights are:

- You have the right to remain silent.
- Anything you say can and will be used against you in a court of law.
- You have the right to have an attorney present before and during any questioning.
- If you cannot afford an attorney, one will be appointed to you by the court free of charge.

If the police detain and interrogate a person without reading them their Miranda Rights, their defense attorney can and should bring a motion (a legal request) to have the court suppress (declare unusable) any statement the person made to the police. This is a powerful tool when it results in entire confessions being thrown out of court.

2. The 1538.5 Motion:

The most common Suppression Motion is known as the 1538.5. This is another reference to the California Penal Code. Penal Code 1538.5 says that when a police officer illegally searches a person or place, the court must declare any evidence found as a result of that illegal action to be inadmissible (unusable) in court. This is a powerful tool when it results in narcotics, weapons, or other extremely necessary evidence being thrown out of court.

3. The Due Process Motion:

This is an all-purpose, catchall motion. Any time law enforcement does anything that violates the United States Constitution, any evidence that they obtain as a result of doing that unconstitutional thing can be thrown out by the judge.

The two most common places where I have used and seen this motion used is in the context of illegal interrogations and suggestive photo-lineups.

Illegal Interrogations:

Even if the cops read the defendant his/her Miranda Rights, an interrogation can be illegal. Obviously the most blatantly illegal interrogation is the "Third Degree," where a defendant is tortured until they confess.

Less obvious, but just as illegal, are cases where the police bribe or threaten people with other things (for instance, lying that they will get to go home if they confess, or threatening to arrest family members or take the suspect's children away if they don't confess).

In extreme enough cases, the very length of the interrogation (I have seen 12-hour interrogations) can be enough to be considered illegal, where the police are obviously trying to "break" the suspect's will through continued harassment.

In all of these illegal interrogations the suspect's statements are involuntary. It is unfair for the government to use involuntary statements against a person, and it thus violates the person's rights to Due Process of Law (basically meaning the right to a fair trial).

A good defense attorney will get these statements deemed inadmissible.

Suggestive Photo-Lineups:

The live photo-lineup made famous by movies and television is rarely, if ever, used in modern times. What is almost always used instead is the much less accurate photo-lineup. The photo-lineup usually presents a witness with pictures of six people, one of which is the suspect, and asks the witness if any of those people is the person who committed the crime. Ideally the six people should look somewhat alike, or at least they should all look different.

Ideally the police should not comment on the photos or attempt to persuade the witness to pick any particular photo. Ideally, in fact, (and this has been suggested for many years), a police officer not related to the case who does not know who the suspect is should perform all photo-lineups with witnesses. That would be fair and would promote truth. Too many police officers don't care about that, however, for it to actually happen everywhere.

In the real world, police often make suggestive lineups such as showing five black and white photos and one color photo (of the defendant), or showing five men with hair and one bald man, or showing four white men and one obviously Hispanic man, or immediately asking the witness to circle and sign the photo when they pick the "correct" one, but frowning and asking "are you sure" when they pick the "incorrect" one.

I HAVE SEEN COPS DO ALL OF THESE THINGS. Some cops have no shame, and you need a defense counsel who will meet them with force, show the courts how dirty they are, and demand that their dirty evidence be suppressed. It is unfair to the defendant for the prosecutor to use a dirty cop's dirty photo ID, and a good judge will prevent them from doing it on Due Process grounds if presented with a well-written motion from defense counsel.

Why would a prosecutor dismiss a case?

There are several possible reasons why a prosecutor may decide that criminal charges against a defendant should be dismissed. Some of the reasons include:

1. The evidence they needed to prove guilt was suppressed by the judge (see above).
2. The prosecutor learns that there is very strong evidence that the defendant is not guilty.
3. The prosecutor learns that their evidence that the defendant IS guilty is not as strong as they thought.
4. The defendant decides to cooperate with law enforcement against other defendants in exchange for having his own case reduced or dismissed.

Numbers 2 and 3, above, deserve some additional discussion. It has been observed by me that poor defense attorneys read the police reports and think they know what happened in their client's case. Average defense attorneys read the police reports, then ask their client what happened, and after that, they think they know what happened in their client's case. Good defense attorneys know that in most criminal cases they need to have a good investigator look for all of the evidence that the police either missed or willfully failed to mention in their reports.[5]

Convincing a prosecutor to dismiss a case because there is a very good chance they will lose in front of a jury is a beautiful thing. Prosecutors are afraid to lose jury trials. The reason that prosecutors are afraid to lose jury trials is that prosecutors all work for the district attorney, who is elected and must stand for re-election. One of the things that these politicians love to brag about is their "win-loss" record. Any underling that brings down the district attorney's win-loss record may find themselves out of a job.

---

[5] I have seen plenty of both in my time.

Chapter 6

Understanding Case Settlement and Plea Bargains

HOW ARE CASES "SETTLED," AND WHAT IS A PLEA BARGAIN?

First, let's identify who does what in the criminal justice system.

> *"In the criminal justice system, the people are represented by two separate yet equally important groups: the police, who investigate crime, and the district attorneys, who prosecute the offenders. These are their stories."* ::bong bong::

This is the opening dialogue to the famous crime drama *Law and Order*, and it is correct. Cases typically start when police officers investigate a crime and make an arrest. After this, the case is sent to the district attorney's office and given to a prosecutor who is responsible for filing charges and eventually taking the case to trial.

It is the district attorney's office, not the police department, that decides whether or not criminal charges will be brought and, if so, what charges specifically will be brought. Years ago, when I was a prosecutor, I spent a great deal of time reading police reports and filling out charging documents.

Many arrests do not lead to criminal charges. Oftentimes, the police have sufficient evidence to make an arrest, but the prosecutor doesn't have sufficient evidence to get a conviction at trial. An ethical prosecutor (and there ARE a few left out there) will not file charges if they don't believe they have enough admissible evidence to win in front of a jury.

How does the prosecutor decide what charges to bring?

For every violation of law, there is a Penal Code Section that gives the "elements" (parts) of the law and describes what a person must do to be in violation of that law. For example: Robbery is a violation of California Penal Code 211. The elements of robbery are that a person:

1. Takes the personal property of another
2. Through force or fear

If the police report shows that there is evidence to prove beyond a reasonable doubt to a jury that the defendant committed those acts, the prosecutor will (or at least should) file those charges.

Choosing what charges to bring gets more complicated when the defendant's actions fulfill the element requirements for multiple offenses of differing severity. For example: Albert stabs Bob in the shoulder with a sharpened stick. Bob survives. Albert's actions have certainly met the element requirements for simple assault, a misdemeanor, but also for assault with a deadly weapon, a felony, and possibly for mayhem, a more serious felony, or even possibly (though probably not) attempted murder, a very serious felony.

The above is a simplification of the kind of choices that prosecutors make every day in deciding what charges to bring against a defendant. In many cases, if not most, they have a great deal of discretion to decide to bring more or less serious charges depending on what they think the case is worth.

In a perfect world, prosecutors everywhere would decide to file more serious charges in cases of more serious wrongdoing and less serious charges in less serious cases of wrongdoing. In reality, most prosecutors file the most serious offense that they can arguably say the defendant's actions fall under.

Why do they do this? They do it so that they can begin the **plea bargain** process from a position of perceived (if not actual) strength. If a defendant is told that he is being charged with attempted murder and is facing a term of life in prison, they are more likely to accept a plea bargain, which allows them to plead to assault with a deadly weapon (a crime with a maximum sentence of 4 years in prison).

Had the prosecutor started by properly charging the defendant with what the case was worth (assault with a deadly weapon), the defendant would be under much less pressure to plead guilty. This is an unethical prosecutorial weasel tactic that a good defense attorney will recognize for what it is.

A prosecutor recently tried to pull this dirty tactic on one of my clients. I set the case for trial, knowing that no jury in the world would convict Albert of attempted murder and that the prosecutor would look like a fool in public for even asking. My client was given the opportunity to plead guilty to a misdemeanor at the next court date.

What is a plea bargain?

A plea bargain is an agreement between the defense attorney (on behalf of the defendant), the prosecutor (on behalf of the district attorney who nominally represents "the people"), and the judge (on behalf of the California Judiciary, which nominally represents "the interests of justice").

Why do the judge and the prosecutor want to settle cases?

Each of the above players has powers to barter with. The defendant has the power to plead guilty or demand a trial. The prosecutor has the power to change what the defendant is charged with. The judge has the power to sentence the defendant (within a range set by statute) if the defendant pleads guilty.

The defendant's power to demand a trial may seem like a very small power, but often it is not. To begin, it is important to know that the VAST majority of criminal cases are settled by plea bargain. They NEED to be. If the VAST majority of criminal cases were not settled by plea bargain and even HALF of those people accused of crimes demanded a trial, the entire California court system would grind to a halt and collapse under its own weight.

The judge needs to clear his "calendar" (the list of cases he is supposed to be dealing with), and he needs defendants to plead guilty for this to happen. The prosecutor often has similar motivations to settle cases. Trials are a lot of work, and many district attorneys' offices operate under the stupid system of simply assigning every prosecutor the same number of cases regardless of how much work goes into them.

Prosecutors are also (as explained earlier) afraid of losing. If your lawyer can convince the prosecutor that they might lose, they will give a great offer to save themselves the risk of getting fired after a not-guilty verdict.

What can the prosecutor do for me?

Almost anything. Prosecutors can dismiss the case, but that is rare. It is far more common for the prosecutor to agree to change what the defendant is charged with to a less serious crime with a lesser sentence range, as long as the defendant will agree to plead guilty to this new charge.

What can the judge do for me?

Not quite as much. Again, as we discussed above, the judge can dismiss the case in certain rare circumstances, but what is much more common is that the judge will give an "Indicated Sentence." An "Indicated Sentence" is a promise from the judge that if the defendant pleads guilty, the judge will give a certain sentence (obviously less than the maximum).

What does a plea bargain look like?

Take our example above. Say that Albert was charged with attempted murder. The case comes to court. The prosecutor, defense attorney, and judge all talk in the judge's chambers. The defense attorney says that his client will plead guilty to misdemeanor battery. The prosecutor replies that they will allow a plea to Mayhem . . . eventually they agree that a charge of assault with a deadly weapon is acceptable to them both.

The judge is then given the opportunity to give an Indicated Sentence. On a conviction for assault with a deadly weapon, the judge can sentence Albert to felony probation and up to 365 days in the county jail, or he can sentence him to prison for 2, 3, or 4 years.

The defense attorney presses the judge, explaining that Albert will only plead guilty if he can do his time in an out-of-custody program (which is only available if he is placed on felony probation). Defense counsel explains that Albert has no prior history, has a good standing in the community, and was partially justified based on the victim's bad actions toward him prior to the stabbing.

The judge agrees to a sentence of 365 days in jail and 3 years' probation. Everyone is (relatively) happy. The judge moves the case off his desk. The prosecutor gets to claim a win for his boss, and the defendant does not have to risk spending years in prison if he is convicted at trial.

Should I plea-bargain my case?

No one can give you an answer to this question without first reading the police reports, talking to the defendant, sending out an investigator to gather more evidence, and then meeting with the prosecutor and the judge.

Far too many bad lawyers simply jump on whatever first offer is made without pressing their advantage and negotiating hard for the best possible resolution.[6] Often this means that cases need to go to trial. Some prosecutors are unreasonable. Some judges are unreasonable. You need to be willing, and you need to have a lawyer who is willing, to go to trial if that is the correct tactical decision.

---

[6] Your lawyer should be the one MAKING the offers, not simply relaying to you what the prosecutor wants.

In some cases, no offer could be good enough. If you KNOW that the government won't be able to show the jury proof beyond a reasonable doubt of your guilt, you should go to trial. I have often had the joy of telling prosecutors that my client will "accept a dismissal and waive the apology" when asked what we were "looking for in settlement."

Chapter 7

When Should You Hire a Lawyer?

SHOULD I HIRE A LAWYER?

What can I do? This is the anguished question that most people are frantically asking themselves when either they or a loved one is accused of a crime. How do I make this better? How do I avoid making it worse? Unfortunately, the answer can be extremely frustrating. The truth is that you can do very little other than obtain the help of a good lawyer.

Now you may be saying to yourself, "What about talking to the witnesses or the supposed victim?" and "If I could only explain myself, I'm sure everything would be all right."

This is a terrible idea. Even if you know who the victim is, and even if you were allowed to talk to them, you are taking an enormous risk by trying to do so. The reason that this is so risky is because **it is a felony offense to attempt to dissuade a witness from testifying and a felony STRIKE offense to threaten a witness.** And you may say to yourself that you don't intend to threaten or dissuade anyone, but you don't know how that person may misinterpret what you say and do. You may intend to do nothing inappropriate and still find yourself facing very serious charges because the victim either misunderstands you or simply decides to lie to get you into trouble. This is a task that you want to leave to your attorney's investigator.

Every serious criminal defense lawyer has at least one, and more likely, several private investigators, that do work for them. Most of these private investigators are former police officers. These professional investigators go out and find witnesses and speak with them on behalf of the client.

Most often this involves getting information about what happened, but sometimes this includes getting witnesses to give their support to a particular plea deal that is beneficial to the defendant. Private investigators are experts at doing these things. They know what questions to ask, they know how to get people to open up to them, and they know how to back off when that is the best thing to do. I've spent more than 10 years practicing law, and I NEVER talk to a witness without at least having a private investigator present. For a layperson to do so would be to invite disaster.

The "pro per" or "pro se" defendant

"Can I represent myself in court? After all, no one cares about this case the way I do, and I don't think anyone else can tell my story like I can."

Alternatively, "Can I represent my wife, or brother, or friend? I'm pretty smart, and I think I can do a better job than any hired-gun attorney can."

First of all, let me say, and I say this with all sincerity, that I respect your bravery and your commitment to justice. Most people are petrified by the idea of public speaking and are extremely intimidated by courtrooms. It is the rare person who has the guts to want to get up and fight it out with a professional attorney (the prosecutor). That being said, if you have been charged with a crime, it is all but suicidal to represent yourself,[7] and unless you are a licensed attorney, you will not be allowed to represent anyone else.

---

[7] A defendant who represents himself is referred to as a "pro per" or "pro se" defendant in legal speak.

You will often hear me making parallels between doctors and lawyers. We are both professionals doing very complex jobs, trying to help people who are in desperate need and facing very serious consequences if the right steps aren't taken to protect our patients/clients. Defending yourself against criminal charges would be tantamount to performing your own emergency surgery after being shot.

1. First of all, you are not objective. Because you are involved in your case, this is an emotional thing for you. It should be! This is your life we're talking about! But lacking objectivity is a weakness when it comes to presenting a case in court. You need someone with a clear head making decisions based on experience and expertise, not on fear, anger, or any other gut reaction.

You may be saying to yourself, "*That isn't me. I can be objective. I can keep it together.*" And maybe you can. Most people can't. Medical doctors are not allowed to treat friends and family members who come into their hospitals because the American Medical Association knows that caring about a patient (as a family member does) is less important than having a surgeon who is clearheaded and able to make unemotional decisions. If I were charged with a crime, I would hire another lawyer to represent me. Is this because I think there are lawyers who are better than me? No, it isn't (modesty is not a virtue among trial attorneys). It's because I know that a professional needs to be objective, and the only way to achieve that is to not be involved in the case except as an advocate for a party.

2. Second of all, you do not understand the law. I mean no disrespect when I say this. You don't understand how to perform heart surgery either (unless you are a heart surgeon), and the two jobs require about the same level of technical knowledge.

Now, a good attorney, just like a good surgeon, will make an effort to teach their patients/clients as much about the process they are about to go through as they can handle. I have found through years of experience that when my clients are able to understand the basic laws that apply to their case, they are better able to assist in their defense, make good decisions about how their case will proceed, and perhaps most importantly to the clients, have the greatest peace of mind and lowest stress during their court ordeal. This is why I wrote this book in the first place!

You may be one of those people who says, "How important can the law really be? This isn't a complicated case. I'm not Martha Stewart charged with securities fraud; I'm charged with robbery (or DUI, or some other fairly straightforward offense). All I need to do is to explain myself to the jury and things will be fine."

You are wrong. Respectfully, you're wrong. The rules of evidence are complicated, so much so that actual lawyers and even a few judges fail to understand the harder parts. There are rules surrounding what questions you can and cannot ask.

- Leading questions are not allowed, except they might be in some cases.
- Hearsay is not allowed, except that there are numerous exceptions to the hearsay rule.
- Questions that lack foundation are not allowed, and if you don't know what that means, you are in good company with several lawyers and judges I know.
- Character evidence may or may not be allowed.
- Compound questions are not allowed.
- Questions that call for a narrative are not allowed and, of course,
- You are not allowed to ask questions about subjects that have been ruled inadmissible during in-limine (pre-trial) arguments.

There are separate rules regarding what physical evidence may be presented to the jury, in what way, having been marked by the clerk of the court in what way, and with what notice to the prosecution.

There are separate rules regarding what notice you are required to give the prosecution of the witnesses you intend to call.

Not only do you need to understand all of these rules in order to get in your own evidence, you need to have an intimate understanding of these rules in order to prevent the prosecutor, who is a trained trial lawyer, from getting in evidence that they shouldn't be allowed to get in.

This leaves out the inevitable discussion of what jury instructions should be read (and with what modifications) and what you can and cannot say in the opening and closing statement, which all require an understanding of the elements of the offense you are charged with and any lesser included offenses . . . I think you get the idea.

"But I'm smart," you say. *"I can learn all of those rules before my trial."* Again, I admire your hutzpah, but that is very unlikely.

But even if that were true, there is always the fact that . . .

3. You have no experience in a courtroom. Answer this question for yourself: you've just been charged with murder. You have a choice of hiring two lawyers. Lawyer number 1 graduated at the top of his class from Stanford Law School and passed the California Bar Exam with a near perfect score . . . yesterday. Lawyer number 2 graduated from a no-name law school 10 years ago, worked for 3 years as a deputy district attorney, and spent the last 7 years running his own law practice where he has completed dozens of trials including several murders.[8]

Or imagine the same questions with doctors. Say that you need to have heart surgery done. Surgeon number 1 just graduated at the top of his class at John's Hopkins University . . . last week. You will be his first surgery. Surgeon number 2 graduated from a no-name medical school ten years ago and has successfully performed this operation dozens of times, including several times in the last 6 months.

Whom did you pick? Was there ever even any doubt? Of course not. Experience is important; we know this instinctively . . . when we are talking about other people.

---

[8] I myself am in the middle, having graduated in the top half of a good law school (Loyola Los Angeles) and having 10 years of experience with a certification from the California Bar as a Certified Criminal Law Specialist.

Now, the fact is that experience is important . . . up to a point. The more experienced lawyer is NOT always the best lawyer. I see lawyers every day that have 20 or more years of experience . . . doing the wrong things. Experience is not sufficient to make for a good trial attorney, but it is absolutely necessary.

Beyond learning all of the technical rules through repetition and varied analysis over time, there are other non-legal intangibles that a trial attorney learns over time. These intangibles include how to speak to a judge, jury, and prosecutor to get the best results out of each, how to pick a jury, how to deliver an opening and closing statement well, and even how to question different types of witnesses (police, expert, and civilian) in different ways to achieve the best results.

Trial litigation is like medical practice. I've said that a few times and will continue with these comparisons, but both are also a little like playing a sport. No matter how much you've read, no matter how much you've watched, until you get out there and swing a racquet a few thousand times, a tennis player you will never be.

Wrap-up—A fool for a client

Every lawyer I know has stories of watching pro per[9] defendants get slaughtered in court. I have several, but this one should suffice to make the point.

I tried a case once where I represented a defendant charged with possession for sale and cultivation of marijuana, along with manufacturing concentrated cannabis. His co-defendant, who lived with him, was charged with the same offenses, along with two additional misdemeanor charges of child endangerment. She decided to represent herself.

---

[9] Pro per is lawyer slang. It is a shortened form of the Latin "*in propria persona*," literally meaning "for one's self." A defendant who represents themselves without a lawyer is said to be a "pro per."

In general, this was not a dumb woman. She was able to read and write well and was, I would estimate, of above-average intelligence. She got embarrassingly slaughtered. She wrote motions to the court that made sense, but got all of the legal arguments wrong, and they were immediately denied. She tried to call witnesses at trial, but had not given the prosecution notice of the witnesses, so they were not allowed to testify.

She was stopped multiple times during her opening and closing arguments because whatever she was saying was something she wasn't allowed to say. Her attempts to question the witnesses were long and painful and, most importantly, futile. Slaughter is the only appropriate word.

At the end of the trial, my client, who was more culpable for everything that had happened, was given a split decision by being found not guilty of the most serious charge against him and was sentenced to 230 days for the lesser charge. The co-defendant, on the other hand, was found guilty of every charge brought against her and was given a sentence of 4 years in the state prison. These two clients were tried AT THE SAME TIME by the SAME JURY.

The old cliché is true. A person who acts as their own lawyer has a fool for a client.

Is it worth it to hire a private lawyer, or should I save my money and use the public defender?

This is a perfectly reasonable question. Having dispensed with the suicidal idea of representing yourself, you need to decide whether to trust the public defender or to hire someone who will work for you to represent you. Here again, I would liken the practice of law to the practice of medicine. Doctors and lawyers are both professionals providing a service. Both services can be complex or simple, depending on the circumstances. Both doctors and lawyers deal with people whose problems can lead to life-changing damage if they are not dealt with correctly.

In the medical world, there are many very good doctors who work for free clinics.[10] Many (though if we are going to be honest, far from most) of the doctors found in free clinics are as smart, caring, and competent as any doctor you could hire.

When I get sick, I don't go to the free clinic.

Why not? Because the people who work at the free clinic are overworked, underpaid, and are forced to work in less than ideal conditions with substandard tools. I know for a fact that I will most likely not see a doctor, but rather get handed off to a nurse who will do 98% of the work on the case. I may spend at most a few minutes with a doctor who will be rushing to see the next patient and for that reason will be unable to talk to me about what's wrong or explain to me what needs to be done. The doctor might be good, but he will miss possibly vital facts about my illness because he is rushing, which will mean that I won't get the correct treatment.

And the doctor probably isn't very good. This might be one of the "true believer" doctors who dedicate their life to public service despite the personal loss of income, but more likely, this is a doctor who either is just out of medical school and in need of experience (which he hopes to get using me) or simply isn't good enough at what he does to either run or get hired in private practice. If I have a simple case, all of that might not make a difference . . . but what if I don't? What if this guy's lack of knowing . . . or caring . . . means that a serious issue gets missed?

The process for me will involve long waits, a frustrating lack of communication, and the frightening knowledge that if I had paid a private doctor I would very likely get better medical treatment. I would surely feel better about the whole thing.

Draw your own comparisons with the Public Defender's Office.

---

[10] In my Rotary Group, we have just finished honoring one such doctor who grew up abandoned by his family working in the fields in Porterville and became an excellent family doctor serving his former community.

Chapter 8

Understanding How Bail and Bonds Work

How does bail work and should I bail out? or
Should I post bail for my loved one?

What is "bail"?

Bail refers to money that is given to the court to hold until a case ends. When the court receives this money, it will release the defendant so that they can remain at liberty as the trial progresses, rather than have to spend that entire time in the county jail.

If the defendant makes all of their court appearances, whoever posted the bail will have that money given back to them when the case ends. A case ends when the defendant is either acquitted (found not guilty) or sentenced.

What is a "bond"?

For our purposes, a bond is something that is given to ensure the completion of a promise. When the promise is kept, the bond is returned. You may have heard it said of a particularly trustworthy person that "their word is their bond." What this means is that the person is staking their reputation for telling the truth on their promise and that no other insurance is considered necessary. Sadly, in most criminal cases, the judge will not allow the defendant's word to be their bond and will instead require bail.

NOTE: When a specific object is given as the bond for the promise of repayment of a debt, this is generally referred to as "collateral." If you need to hire a bail bondsman, they may require that you put up collateral (such as a house or a car) as part of their contract with you.

What has to happen before I can be bailed out?

After a person is arrested, they are taken to the sheriff's department to be "booked" into the county jail. The "booking" process (literally meaning the process to put the defendant "in the books" of the jail, or more modernly, into the computer system) takes anywhere from less than an hour to several hours, depending on when and where a person is arrested and booked.

The booking process involves taking a picture of the defendant, fingerprinting them, then running a background check to see if the defendant has any outstanding warrants. Assuming that the defendant does not have any outstanding warrants and they have been arrested for something other than a serious and violent felony, they will immediately become eligible to be bailed out according to the county bail schedule (more on this below). Once booked in, the defendant will be allowed to make a phone call.

How do I get bailed out?

There are two ways to "make bail." If someone, be it the defendant or the friends and family of the defendant, is willing and able to give the court the entire amount of bail to hold until the end of the case, they can do so, and the defendant will be released. This is very rare. It is much more common for the defendant to need to employ a bail bondsman.

A bail bondsman, in exchange for a fee and often the attachment of collateral, will post bail for the defendant. A bail bondsman, in essence, issues a large, albeit relatively short-term, loan to the defendant and/or his friends and family. Typically, the bail bondsman will charge a fee of 10% of the total bail amount. This money is paid to the bondsman in exchange for the loan.

If the defendant "jumps bond" or fails to appear as scheduled for their court appearance, the bail bondsman is given a certain amount of time to find the defendant and bring them back to court before the bail bondsman's investment is forfeited to the court. This encourages the bail bondsman to use private detectives who, under the law, are given the power to arrest bail jumpers and bring them to the court. These private detectives are often referred to as "bounty hunters," though this name has not been accurate for some time in the United States.

A NOTE ON COLLATERAL: Collateral refers to something of value that a person gives to the bondsman to hold on to until the bondsman gets his money back from the court at the end of the case. Typically, this is the deed to some property owned by the defendant or the friends and family of the defendant. If the defendant then fails to appear and the bond is forfeited, the bondsman will keep the collateral as payment for the loss of the money they put up.

Does every person who is charged with a crime need to post a bail bond?

No. The law gives the police a choice whether to book people who are charged with certain offenses into the county jail or not. If a person is booked into the county jail and charges are filed within 72 hours, the person will need to either make bail or convince a judge to let them out on what lawyers call their "own recognizance" (essentially their good word that they will return).

For most misdemeanors, the police are not required to book the defendant into the jail, and different police agencies have different policies regarding how officers can or must use that discretion. For example, almost all police agencies will cite and release (rather than arrest and book) people accused of petty theft or possession of narcotics (both misdemeanors). Almost all police agencies, however, have a policy that requires their officers to arrest and book any person accused of domestic violence (even as a misdemeanor) or any felony.

Most jurisdictions allow the police officer to decide whether to cite or arrest a person charged with simple assault. Existing in a somewhat middle ground are the cases of people accused of being drunk in public, being under the influence of illegal narcotics, or DUI. The police are generally required to arrest and take the person into custody (unless they can be immediately released to a responsible, sober adult), but they will typically be held for only a few hours (in a drunk tank) until they "sober up" and can be cited out.

If I do have to post bail, what are some ways to reduce the amount a bail bondsman will charge?

- Hire an attorney — Many bond agencies will give up to a 20% reduction off their rates to a person who has a private criminal defense attorney representing them. The existence of a private attorney shows that the defendant is stable and is unlikely to jump bond.
- Posting collateral such as a home — If the bond company can get someone to offer collateral like a home to secure the bond, they will lower the amount that they charge.
  - What does this mean? Say that the bond is $100,000, and say, for example, that the defendant's Grandpa Joe is willing to list his home for collateral on the bond. The bail bondsman may be willing to reduce the amount they charge. The reason for this is simple. If the defendant jumps bond, and the court takes the $100,000 that the bail bondsman has posted away from him, the bail agent will promptly foreclose on Grandpa Joe's house to pay back the amount lost.

Will I have to pay the entire 10% to the bail bondsman up front?

Maybe not. The bail agent (employee of the bail bondsman) wants to make a sale, but the bail bondsman also wants to minimize his own risk. The answer to the question of whether you're offered a payment plan and of what type will be available to you depends on a number of factors including:

- Your credit rating
- Your income
- Your ability and willingness to post collateral

In most cases you should be prepared to put down at least half of the payment to the bail agent before they will be willing to post bond for the defendant. That means 5% of the total bail, or in our $100,000 example, $5,000.

A NOTE ABOUT BOND EXPIRATION: Bail bonds typically last only 1 year. The vast majority of criminal cases will resolve within that year but not all. If your matter takes more than 1 year, you may need to contract with your bail agent to post a new bond.

What happens if the defendant posts bail and then fails to appear?

Two things will happen if the defendant fails to appear in court:

1. The court will put out a warrant for the arrest of the defendant.
2. A 180-day countdown will begin until bail is forfeited.

What does this mean?

1. In terms of the warrant, it means that if the defendant comes into contact with law enforcement for any reason involving a warrant check (for example ANY traffic stop) they will be arrested. It is also possible that police will be sent to look for and arrest the defendant.
2. In terms of the countdown, it means that if the defendant does not appear in court within 6 months of the date of the failure to appear, the court gets to keep the money that it was given to hold. This gives the person who posted the bond a strong incentive to bring the defendant back to court.

What kind of forms will I need to fill out to hire a bail bondsman?

- Financial Disclosure
- Contract

- Indemnification

The bondsman is going to want to know that you are able to pay them back and for this reason will ask for your financial records. This may include requests for a copy of your latest paycheck, a copy of your most recent tax returns, a written breakdown of all of your assets and debts, and a summary of your current spending habits.

After looking at your financial disclosure and determining that they are willing to contract with you to post the bond that you want, the bail bondsman will have you sign a contract. The contract will include terms such as:

- That you make payment on scheduled dates
- That you keep in contact with the defendant and inform the bail bondsman of the defendant's whereabouts if requested
- That you sign an indemnification

What is an indemnification?

For our purposes here, indemnification means that the person contracting with the bail bondsman (and anyone required to co-sign) is saying that if the bail bondsman loses any money as a result of this contract (whether it be the necessity to send private detectives to look for the defendant or pay the court because the defendant has failed to appear, etc.), they will pay that money back to the bail bondsman. The result of all of this is to put the negative results of the defendant's failure to appear not on the bail bondsman but on the defendant and his friends and family.

What is a co-signer?

For our purpose here, a co-signer is a second person who also assumes the duties of the contract, including the indemnification.

How is the amount of bail set?

Each county has its own bail schedule that lists the amount of money that needs to be posted in order to be bailed out after a person is arrested. Different amounts are set for each possible criminal charge.

The Tulare County bail schedule can be found at:
http://www.tularesuperiorcourt.ca.gov/docs/TCSC_BailSched.pdf

The King's County bail schedule can be found at:
http://www.kings.courts.ca.gov/depts/criminal/Criminal_Main.asp

The Fresno County bail schedule can be found at:
http://www.fresno.courts.ca.gov/_pdfs/UniformBailSchedule2017.pdf

Am I stuck with the bail schedule?

Not necessarily. The bail schedule is used to determine the bail at the time of arrest and will stay in effect until at least the first court appearance. At the first court appearance, the judge may decide to keep the bail set according to the schedule or either raise it (usually at the request of the district attorney's office) or lower it (at the request of the defendant or the defendant's attorney).

What is the one sure-fire way to get a request for bail reduction denied?

The one guaranteed way to get a request for a bail reduction denied is for a defendant simply to make the request and then not say anything else. I have seen this happen a discouraging number of times while in court defending my better-prepared clients. The defendant's case will be called for arraignment, he or she will come up to the podium, they will enter a plea of not guilty, and then they will ask the judge, "Can I get an O.R.?" What is going through the mind of such a person is a mystery to me.

Why in the WORLD they believe such a request would be granted without giving the judge the slightest reason to do so, I can't imagine. The judge is not going to look for reasons to lower the defendant's bail. If he even opens the file in response to such a request, it will only be to glance at the defendant's history to see if he wants to raise bail and to check that the defendant's bail is set according to the bail schedule before denying the request.

A twin to this failed non-strategy is the defendant who asks the judge to let them out of custody loudly and confidently, proclaiming that because they didn't do it, they should be released. I understand where these defendants are coming from, and I sympathize. Being arrested and held in jail is one of the most traumatic experiences most people will ever face. Add to this the injustice of being arrested falsely, and it's almost too much to bear without making an outburst. The absolute and painful truth is that it isn't going to help.

In setting bail, the judge is required by law to assume that the defendant is guilty of the crimes they are charged with. The judge at the arraignment is not going to read the police reports, he is not going to review the evidence against you, and he is not going to be swayed by anything you say about the weakness of the government's case. Every judge in this situation, EVERY ONE OF THEM, will respond in the same way. They will tell the defendant that if they are innocent, they should take their case to trial, and that is why the court system exists. They will then deny their request to lower bail and set the next court date.

What other serious mistakes can a defendant make at a bail reduction hearing?

One of the most, if not THE most important reason to have an attorney represent a defendant at every court appearance is that everything that is said in court is written down by the court reporter, and everything the defendant says "can and will be used against them." This is something else I have seen a disheartening number of times while appearing in court with my better prepared clients: a defendant will get up and ask the judge to lower their bail. In the process, they will begin discussing their case with the judge because they think that if they can only explain to the judge what happened, the judge will release them.

Not only does the judge not release them, but while they are talking, the defendant winds up confessing to facts that the prosecution probably would never have been able to prove had they remained silent. A defendant should never argue their own bail motion. They will always be best served by hiring a private defense attorney who will have the time and knowledge to make the best argument possible for them, but even if they must wait several days to have an overworked public defender make the argument, they are better served to do so than to attempt to make the argument themselves. There are simply too many pitfalls that a person without legal training can fall into when speaking in court.

What factors are taken into consideration when a judge decides whether or not to lower bail?

- The most important thing to know is that the California Constitution, Article 1, Section 12(c) gives each person accused of a crime the right to "reasonable bail." There is a complicated network of statutory and case law that has been written on the subject of what is "reasonable." If an argument can be made to the judge that the scheduled bail is not "reasonable" in your case, the judge will be compelled to lower bail to a "reasonable" amount.
- The two primary factors the judge will use in deciding the amount of "reasonable bail" are the danger the defendant will pose to society if released and the likelihood that the defendant will fail to appear in the future if released.

NOTE: There is an exception to the right to bail. Under Article 12 Section 1 of the California Constitution, if a person is accused of a crime punishable by the death penalty or a serious felony and the likelihood of danger to the public is high, the court can refuse to set a bail, meaning the accused must remain in custody while the case progresses.

What are some of the "bad facts" that a judge will consider (if known) in setting bail?

1. Defendant on probation and/or already on bail:
If the defendant is on probation for another offense or has another open criminal case, this is considered by most judges to be a very

damaging fact, suggesting that bail should be raised above the normal schedule. The reasoning is obvious. It will appear to the court (in the absence of a good argument explaining to the contrary) that the defendant has been given a chance to stay out of trouble and has thrown that chance away by continuing to commit crimes. Such a person, if admitted to bail at all, is likely to face an extreme upward deviation unless some mitigating factors can be explained to the judge. The presence of an attorney for such an argument could literally save the defendant/defendant's friends and family thousands of dollars.

2. Prior record:

Prior convictions, particularly for violent offenses or the same offense that the defendant stands accused of, will suggest to most judges that the defendant's bail should be raised or, at the very least, not lowered. This goes to the number-one factor mentioned above — public safety. What you need to understand is that in the state of California, judges must stand for election every six years. The nightmare of every criminal court judge when setting bail is for them to reduce bail so that a defendant can be released and then to have that defendant commit some heinous crime while out on bond. The judge can almost see the attack ads explaining how they are "soft on crime" and allowed a "dangerous criminal back into the community to re-offend."

Knowing this, if a defendant has an extensive criminal record and expects any chance of their bail being lowered, they need an experienced attorney to allay the judge's fears by explaining why this defendant really isn't a public threat. This is done by arguing all the "good facts" (below) that exist in the defendant's favor, while minimizing the "bad facts" by explaining what actually happened and why many prior convictions are really not as bad as they appear.

3. High-profile crime charges:

There are some offenses that, unfortunately, have a tendency to capture public attention:

- Sex crime charges, especially child molestation charges
- Multiple conviction DUI charges
- Domestic violence charges
- Crimes against the police or other high-profile victims

There isn't anything about these charges that would justify an unusual unwillingness by judges to lower bail or an especially eager tendency to raise bail, but that is the fact of the matter, and you are going to have to deal with it somehow. Sometimes it just requires holding the judge's feet to the fire by demanding a bail reduction hearing, presenting overwhelming evidence of the defendant's suitability to be released, and then demanding that the prosecution or the court either present some rebuttal or do what you ask under the law. The judge doesn't want to lower bail in these cases. They prefer to keep as low a profile as possible, knowing that these cases will likely appear in the news. At the same time, they know they have a job to do. Sometimes my job as a lawyer is to make the man (or woman) in the black robe do their job as a judge.

4. Prior failure to appear or arrest on an old warrant:
The death blow of many requests to lower bail is when the judge looks at the defendant's record and finds that they have been released from custody in the past and then failed to appear as scheduled. Under such circumstances, the judge, understandably, has little faith that the defendant will not do the same thing if they are released this time. The same situation is found when a person is arrested on a warrant for failing to come to court in the past. The instinct of most judges in these situations is to raise bail to cover the increased risk of flight or, at the very least, deny any request to lower bail made without any context.

What are some of the "good facts" that the judge will consider (if known) in setting bail?

1. Prior record:

Obviously, the best-case scenario is to have a defendant with no criminal record, who has never been arrested, and is facing criminal charges for the first time in their life. Under such a circumstance, the judge is likely to find that the defendant poses a minimal risk to society. That doesn't mean the judge will automatically lower their bail just because they ask — the judge will not. It does mean, however, that they start out at less of a disadvantage.

What if the defendant *does* have a criminal record?
The defendant's attorney will need to minimize the damage by explaining how the prior record is not as bad as it appears and how other factors are more important.

For example:
The defendant may have serious felony priors on their record, but they may have pled guilty to those offenses as a result of a plea bargain (rather than a guilty verdict at trial), whereby they were sentenced to little or no time.

Or:
The defendant has a record of convictions for violent offenses or drug offenses, but the convictions are so old that they no longer accurately reflect the defendant's disposition TODAY to commit those crimes. By way of example, a person who has a litany of violent crime convictions from when they were in their teens and early 20s (when they were among the "young and the restless") probably has very little propensity to commit those crimes when they are in their 30s or 40s, let alone their 50s or 60s. It is well known amongst criminal law professionals that tendency towards violence falls exponentially with age.

Along the same lines, a person with a string of 5 to 10-year-old drug convictions has almost certainly cleaned up their lives or there would be more current convictions. Again, the priors don't indicate any current threat to society. Is the judge likely to see this? No, they are not. Without someone to argue the facts to the judge, the judge will glance at the rap sheet, notice there are priors, lump the defendant into the high-risk category, and move on. The judge is busy. He has 50 arraignments to do this morning, and he is only going to give your case as much thought as your attorney makes him or her give.

2. Employment:

Criminal court judges are always happy to see a defendant who has a job, any kind of job. Because of experience with criminals day in and day out, judges' standards are low, and you should play this to your advantage. Having a job both means that a person is responsible and that they are contributing to society in some beneficial way. It also means that they are busy, at least during working hours, and not out getting into trouble. If it is at all possible to have a supervisor write a short letter to the judge saying that they hope the court will release the defendant so they can continue working, that often goes a long way to convincing a judge to lower bail.

Similarly, if the defendant has lived in the jurisdiction of the court for many years, is a member of neighborhood organizations, and has a number of friends and family willing to come to court to show support (more on this below), these things will go to show that the defendant has such strong ties to the community that he would never run away or not appear as scheduled in court.

3. Dependents and other family:

Every judge will tell you that they don't take into consideration whether or not the defendant has family that he or she is responsible for taking care of. Most of them are lying. If nothing else, showing the judge that the defendant has family members that they are responsible for (either financially or in some other way) shows that they are less likely to flee, because they have strong ties to the community.

Non-dependent family members can also make a big difference, particularly if they are willing to come to court on the day of the bail reduction hearing. Such family members can stand up and say to the court (through the defendant's attorney, who will ask each of them to stand in turn and be recognized by the judge) that they are willing to watch over the defendant, make sure that he doesn't get into any more trouble, and drive him to and from his court dates. This is a particularly effective move with younger defendants who have large extended families who live in the area they are being charged in.

I'm giving away a bit of a trade secret here, but the coup de grace here is to the bring in the family members who will actually be posting bail for the defendant and to point them out to the judge, in the presence of the defendant. I had a case once in the city of Porterville where the defendant was charged with a series of gang offenses, whereby his bail had been set at nearly $300,000. I brought in the defendant's grandfather, who was a WWII veteran, wearing his Purple Heart jacket. I had him stand up and explain that he had a little more than $10,000 in savings and that he was willing to put up that money, and his home of 50 years, as collateral to a bail bonds agent if his grandson could be released pending trial. I stood in front of the court and explained that the defendant might be a bad kid who had made bad choices, but that he wasn't about to see his grandpa put out in the street by failing to come back to court. A 10-minute ringing lecture from the judge to the defendant about what horrible things he would do to him if he *did* fail to appear later, bail was reduced by more than two thirds to $75,000.

4. Letters of good character:

One of the most effective means of convincing a judge that a defendant is a good candidate for a reduction in bail is to flood the court with letters of good character from friends, family, co- workers, etc. These letters should all say two things, surrounded by whatever other fluff about the defendant's actual good character the writer can think to say: 1. I will personally see that the defendant has a ride to court and will come with him if necessary. And 2. I don't believe that the defendant is the kind of person who could have committed this crime, and he must be innocent.

I can already hear the objection to this idea: "*WHAT? Didn't you just say that the judge must assume that the defendant is guilty and that you can't legally argue otherwise?"* Yes, I did. And I meant it. But lawyers are often at their best when working in the murky in-between places of the law. As a lawyer, I am not allowed to argue to the judge in a motion to reduce bail that the defendant didn't do it. It isn't legally relevant because of a presumption that I am expected to understand and respect. But the writer of a letter of recommendation isn't expected to know the law. For the writer of a letter of recommendation to say that they don't believe the defendant is guilty is just another way of them saying that they don't think he is a danger to society and that he will appear at all of his further court dates. If the judge also happens to be inundated with the message that the community is convinced of the defendant's innocence . . . well I just can't help that, and most judges can't ignore it.

5. Outside-the-box options:

Occasionally the court will agree to release a defendant (or lower their bail to a level where they can secure their own release) if the defendant is willing to agree to certain terms in the bargain. Some of the things I have seen successfully suggested to courts include:

- The defendant will immediately begin Alcoholics Anonymous or Narcotics Anonymous classes or, in more serious cases, check into a residential treatment center. (In DUI and Drug Offense cases.)
- The defendant will agree to be placed under house arrest pending trial (this is used extensively in King's County but has, so far, not caught on in Tulare County).
- The defendant will give their license to the court and agree not to drive a vehicle pending trial. (In DUI cases.)
- The defendant will abstain from drinking pending trial. (In DUI cases.)
- The defendant will move out of the victim's home but continue to support the victim pending trial. (In domestic violence cases.)
- The defendant will take anger management, parenting, or other classes as ordered by the court. (Domestic violence, child neglect, and various other cases.)

These agreements are to terms that are often similar or identical to those terms that would be imposed as conditions of probation if the defendant were to be convicted of the offense. The judge will almost never suggest these terms as a condition of release and, in some cases, indeed might get in trouble with the Judicial Council were they to do so. If such terms are suggested by the defendant's attorney, however, they often go a long way towards convincing the judge to allow the defendant to be released.

A note on when NOT to request a bail reduction hearing:

Occasionally, because of a variety of factors that any good attorney could spot, bail will be set below where it should be. When this happens, any defendant with the means to do so will be advised by any competent attorney to post bail immediately and get out while the "getting is good."

It is important to realize that bail is initially set by the sheriff's department when the person is booked into the county jail and that they sometimes make mistakes. Some of the reasons that might lead to bail being set lower than it should are:

- The sheriff's department didn't realize that the defendant has a strike prior or some other very serious prior conviction that would lead any reviewing judge to raise their bail.
- The sheriff's department didn't realize that the defendant was on probation, parole, or already out on bail in another case.
- The arresting agency booked the defendant in on charges that are substantially less serious than those the district attorney is likely to actually charge.

In these, and similar, situations, I will tell my clients to post bond BEFORE the arraignment. It is unlikely that the prosecutor will ever look too closely at the bail in a case, and it is almost unheard of for a judge to raise bail without a request from a prosecutor.

The worst thing you could do in a case like this, and one of the pitfalls that awaits those without a good attorney to advise them, is to wait for the arraignment and then ask the court to lower bail. As I said, any competent lawyer will see the sheriff's mistake, and that includes the judge, who will review the defendant's file. Bail will be raised to the appropriate level immediately if the judge then sees the error that the defendant themselves pointed out. Not good.

They say I'm not eligible for bail. Why is that?

There are a few situations where a person cannot be bailed out pending trial. These include:

- You are serving out a sentence for another case.
- You have an immigration hold.
- You have an outstanding warrant in another jurisdiction.
- Someone has requested a 1275 hearing.

As to the first three reasons listed above, what must be remembered is that posting bail only releases a defendant in the case for which it is posted. If the defendant is being held in jail for other reasons not related to the case that they posted bail on, they will still not be released. A person cannot be a "little bit" in jail. It may be possible to bail out on multiple cases, but there are circumstances when a person is held in jail and cannot be bailed out.

If a defendant is serving out a sentence, they will not be released until that sentence is completed. If they are charged with another case while serving that sentence, they will not be eligible for bail on the new case until the sentence on the old case is served. If a person has charges pending in another jurisdiction, they can only bail out if they are able to post bail in that other jurisdiction. This is often complicated by the necessity of clearing a warrant in that other jurisdiction. If a person has an immigration hold, sometimes called an ICE hold (ICE stands for Immigration and Customs Enforcement) this means that they are pending federal charges for being an illegal immigrant. In such a case, they will not be released unless they can also post bail in federal court.

What is a 1275 hearing?

A 1275 hearing refers to California Penal Code Section 1275.1. It is a hearing requested either by the county sheriff or the district attorney, requesting that the court require the defendant to prove that the money used for bail was not illegally obtained. This kind of hearing is generally requested in cases where the defendant is accused of running some sort of illegal business or otherwise illegally obtaining money such as by selling contraband (drugs, guns, etc.) or committing fraud. The idea is that it would be wrong for such a person to use their ill-gotten gains to help secure their release from jail.

At such a hearing, the judge will ask where the money going to the court (if the defendant or their family and friends post the bond themselves) or the money going to pay the bail bondsman's fee (in the case of a bail bond) is coming from.

The good news is that it is very simple, 99% of the time, for an attorney to prevail at these hearings and to show that the money going towards the bond is "clean." The easiest method of doing so is to simply provide that someone other than the client is putting up the money as a gift.

The bad news is that until the hearing is held, the defendant will continue to be held in the county jail.

Why might I not want to bail myself or my loved one out?

1. You don't have the money to pay both a bail bond and an attorney.

This is one of the most emotionally charged questions that I get. Jail is not a nice place. Most of the people in jail think of nothing more often than how to get out of jail. I have seen defendants foolishly accept "deals" that place them at long-term risk in order to get out of jail that day.

I certainly understand the desire to get out of jail as soon as possible. More than that, I feel a particular compassion for family members of an inmate who continually calls, begging them to come up with the money to bail them out so they can come home.

I would strongly suggest, however, that everyone having to make a decision regarding bail consider the following:

If you are in jail, you want to get out. If someone you care about is in jail, you want to get them out. But if you have limited resources, you need to decide where they will do the most good. If you or a loved one is facing a long jail sentence if convicted of a crime and you only have the money to either bail them out or to pay for a private attorney, you are a fool to not choose the attorney. As terrible a thing as it is to spend months and months sitting in the county jail waiting for trial, it is very much worse to spend years and years rotting in the state prison because the public defender didn't have the time, experience, or knowledge necessary to defend you properly.

2. Your loved one needs to spend some time in jail.

There is a sad scene I've seen play out several times in my office. Parents come into my office, and they have an adult child with multiple prior convictions, usually including drug convictions, who has just been arrested, again, and is sitting in the county jail. They hire me to defend their son or daughter, and they hire my bail bondsman to get their son or daughter released from jail. The next meeting gets set to discuss the defendant's case, and there are the parents in my office again . . . without the defendant. Inevitably the parents will give me the excuse that their child gave them that they "had to work" or some other mistruth.

At this point, I think that things are going to go badly and, more times than I care to remember, they have. The defendant will fail to appear in court and have a warrant issued for their arrest, or they will get arrested again for some other offense — or, in two real-world cases of my own, they will end up dead. One client died from a drug overdose and another wrapped his car around a tree while drunk.

There are times, therefore, and they are rare, that I suggest that the family (usually the parents) refuse to bail their kids out until we can get a judge to order them into some kind of treatment program to deal with their underlying issues. This DOES NOT mean throwing your loved one at the mercy of the criminal justice system and hoping that it will "do them some good." It will not. The criminal justice system grinds people up quickly, cheaply, and uncaringly. Our system is not set up to rehabilitate anyone.

55

You absolutely should hire a lawyer to represent your loved one's best interest in court, and you absolutely should never counsel anyone to plead guilty until they have spoken to a lawyer. That being said, it can, on very rare occasions, be in the best interest of a defendant to spend some time in jail.

Chapter 9

Stories from the Law Office of Greg Hagopian

One of the great joys of being a criminal defense attorney is that this job comes with great stories. Many of those stories illustrate some of the important things that I have learned about the criminal justice system and that I hope will help you in understanding your situation going forward. Of course, just as I will when I am one day retelling the glory of YOUR case, I have changed the names and other identifying characteristics of the participants in these stories to protect their privacy.

THE FIGHTER

This is a good story for showing how investigation is crucial to a competent defense attorney.

A while back, I had a client come into my office who was facing two charges of robbery with a knife. If convicted, this person (let's call him Frank) faced a sentence of up to 7 years. What had Frank done wrong? Nothing. Frank wasn't a robber or a thief; he was just in the wrong place at the wrong time.

Here's how it went down: Frank went to a mixed martial arts gym. One day after his workout, Frank stopped at Subway for dinner on his way home. The Subway got robbed that day. After Frank left, a man with a similar build to Frank entered the store and held the two clerks at knifepoint while ordering them to empty the register and give him the money. The police were called and took a report.

Two days later, Frank is still going to the MMA gym, and he stops at Subway again. It's roughly the same hour, and the same two girls are working as clerks. The two girls see Frank, are convinced that this is the man who robbed them, and call the police. The police arrive within minutes. The clerks point Frank out (still standing in line waiting to order his sandwich) and tell the police "That's him!" The police grabbed Frank, unnecessarily threw him to the ground, handcuffed him, and carted him off to jail.

The girls were re-interviewed. They told the police that they were both 100% sure (that's a direct quote) that this was the person who robbed them. They explained how, just one week prior, he came into the store, bought a sandwich, left the store, came back to use the restroom, left again, and then came back in, wearing a mask, to rob them.

Two eyewitnesses. Each is 100% sure they can identify the suspect as the perpetrator. The suspect then brazenly returns to the scene of the crime, two days later. That's pretty good evidence, and if you're feeling a little uneasy for the fate of our friend Frank, you aren't alone. Frank had plenty to be worried about at this point.

I asked Frank, "Did you go anywhere afterwards where you could have been video-recorded?" "I think so," he said, a little confused. "My neighbor has a video camera outside of his house. It may have recorded me walking up to my parent's house."

As it turned out, the neighbor's camera did capture Frank getting home the day of the robbery, and we were able to get to the neighbors in time to prevent them from recording over the tape. More importantly, as it turned out, the *Subway* sandwich shop had a security camera, which recorded the whole thing.

No one had ever looked at the tape. The recording equipment is locked so that the regular employees can't access it. The two clerks who made the ID hadn't watched the tape. They relied on their memory of a traumatic situation to be accurate. The police officers who arrested Frank and carted him off to jail hadn't watched the tape. They relied on the eyewitness statement as proof that Frank was guilty. To their credit, the police did ask that the manager be contacted and that he have a copy of the tape turned over to them.[11] The district attorney who filed charges against Frank that would ruin his good name and result in his potentially spending years of his life in prison hadn't watched the tape. He relied on the police investigation.

Counsel for the defendant was the first person to think that viewing the actual videotape of the robbery might be necessary. We sent a demand that the police turn the tape over to us, which was (after more time than it should have taken) eventually complied with. Here is what we found:

The tape did indeed show Frank going into Subway, standing in line, and ordering a sandwich. He did then, indeed, leave the store for a brief moment before coming back to use the restroom. And, indeed, a person does come in, shortly after Frank left for the second time, and could be seen on the video holding up the clerks at knifepoint. That person:

- Wore a different shirt than the defendant.
- Wore pants, when the defendant had worn shorts.
- Wore sandals, where the defendant had worn shoes.
- And wore a different baseball cap than the defendant was wearing.

The videotape from Frank's neighbors? It showed him walking up to his parent's house, holding a Subway bag, wearing exactly the same clothes he was wearing when he went into the Subway both times.

In other words, unless Frank had gone to his car, changed clothes completely, gone back into the store, robbed it, changed clothes completely again, and then returned home . . . it was someone else.

---

[11] To their discredit, when they got the tape the next day, they didn't bother to watch it. It wasn't until we pointed out what the tape showed later that they actually played it for themselves.

The day after I received the tape (more than a month after the arrest) I had a defense investigator go to the Subway sandwich shop, meet with the two clerks, and show them the tape. They were horrified. According to the investigator, one of the girls, nearly hyperventilating, kept repeating over again, "Oh my God. Oh my God. I can't believe we had him arrested. I really thought it was him! I really thought it was him."

And I'm sure she did. But despite the fact that she was 100% sure, she was 100% wrong.

It would be dramatic at this point to say that if we didn't have that video evidence, an innocent man would be in prison today! And that might have happened. It certainly would have been more likely, but even had we not had this clear-cut evidence of Frank's innocence, there were other things that a good defense attorney could have done in his case.

For one thing, there are a number of expert witnesses in the state of California who can be used to explain to juries how unreliable eyewitness identification is. There is one such witness (Dr. Robert Shomer) that I have used several times in the last few years with very impressive results. He would have explained how when a witness experiences a traumatic event (like being threatened with a knife and robbed), the faces of people they have seen near that time, or around the scene, tend to blend and be misremembered as the assailant's. He would testify that such high- pressure situations, far from making a person's memory more reliable (i.e., "I'll never forget his face!"), in reality make the witness's memory LESS reliable.

A good defense attorney would also call character witnesses in a case such as Frank's. In fact, during one of the discussions that I had with Frank in my office, he once said in exasperation, "I would never pull a weapon on a woman. If anything, I would have been the person who jumped on that guy to protect those girls."

Having spent some time talking to Frank, I don't doubt that he was telling the truth. He was a very athletic guy who worked out at a fighter's gym. I'm sure I could have gotten a whole group of people who would have been willing to come into court and tell the jury how Frank was a gentle giant who wouldn't ever threaten any woman and would never commit a robbery of anyone.

Needless to say, the robbery charge was dismissed by the prosecution.

THE ASSAULT WEAPON RIDING SHOTGUN

This is a great story for anyone who assumes that most lawyers know the law (they don't).

A young woman, not even 21 years old, came into my office one day after spending several thousand dollars to bail herself and her boyfriend out of the county jail on FELONY charges of possession of an illegal assault weapon. Let's call her Carla. Carla told me about how she was driving her car with her boyfriend in the passenger seat when they got pulled over by the police for speeding (I can assure you this was a pretext stop[12] and the boyfriend in question was a local gang member).

The police pull them over and they see something at the foot of the passenger compartment that makes them nervous. There is an object the size of a rifle, wrapped in a blanket. Carla's boyfriend is on misdemeanor probation, so the police get to search him and his things at will, which they do. The police order both the passenger and driver out of the vehicle. They unwrap the blanket and BINGO, a big, scary, unloaded, Chinese-made SKS semi-automatic rifle is found. Carla is arrested along with her boyfriend for possession of this "illegal assault weapon."

I should tell you that Carla had no idea what type of rifle it was. She hired me to defend her, not having this information, and I went into this case assuming that this was going to be a case of arguing (correctly) to a judge and jury that the driver of a vehicle is not "in possession" of a wrapped firearm possessed by the passenger. This was a good argument, but it turned out to be unnecessary.

---

[12] One of the many technically legal but wholly unethical practices of modern law enforcement is to stop people not because they have done anything wrong, but to harass them by pretending like they have done something wrong.

Doing my job, I actually looked up the California Penal Code Assault Weapons statute. For those who are interested, this can be found in California Penal Code 30510. The statute states in Section (a) (11) that a SKS with a detachable magazine is considered to be an assault weapon. So, I followed up with the district attorney's office to get pictures of the rifle that was seized (as it turns out, illegally), and I found . . . no detachable magazine.

You see, the SKS was manufactured before the invention of the detachable magazine and originally used a method of loading that involved pushing each individual round into the gun through an opening above the chamber. This is the type of gun Carla's gang member boyfriend had, not the much more deadly version with a detachable magazine allowing for quick reloading, which California has classified as an "assault weapon."

I've now found the code and possess the pictures that show my client and her good-for-nothing boyfriend (who is defended by the Public Defender's Office) are innocent. I go to the first court appearance. I tell the prosecutor that the rifle isn't an assault weapon and show her the code and photographs. This young woman takes the copies that I have made for her of the code and the photographs and tells me, in all seriousness, "I'll reduce the charge to misdemeanors for both of them if they plead guilty today."

Now I'm just dumbfounded. "I don't think you heard me," I replied. "The rifle is not an assault weapon."

"I'll have to check that out. The officer said it was an assault weapon. And even if it isn't, it's still a felony to have an unregistered firearm in a vehicle."

Now I remember being a young deputy district attorney, and so despite the fact that I just gave this baby-lawyer all of the information she needs to understand what she should have worked out for herself had she been competent . . . I try to sympathize and keep things civil. "Okay," I say, taking a deep breath.

"First, it is perfectly legal in the state of California to have an unloaded rifle in your vehicle. Some vehicles even have gun racks for this purpose. The law you are thinking of only applies to loaded rifles or handguns.

Look, why don't we put this case over two weeks, and you can look at what I've given you and talk to your supervisor."

Having completed small talk with the deputy district attorney, I go to try and find the public defender who is representing the co-defendant. Let's call him Mr. P. I manage to find and flag down Mr. P, who is in the normal frenzied rush that most public defenders find themselves in every day.[13]

Of necessity I try to be brief. "Good morning, Mr. P. I'm representing Carla, and I understand you —"

He cuts in. "Is your client going to plead?"

I try to not be annoyed at the interruption. "I don't think so, no," I respond. "Have you seen the pictures of the rifle?"

"No, the police didn't take pictures of the gun.[14] Have you talked to the D.A. this morning?"

"Yes, I . . ."

"She's making a misdemeanor offer for the both of them. I'm telling my guy to jump on it. He's on probation, and if he gets convicted of a felony —"

It is now time for me to interrupt. "IT'S NOT AN ASSAULT WEAPON."

He stops and blinks a few times. "How do you know?" And so, I explain to him the law, the pictures, and the brief discussion I've already had with the baby-district attorney.

In the end, the baby-D.A. spoke to her supervisor, who explained that I was right about it being legal to carry an unloaded rifle in a vehicle (though I wouldn't recommend it), and she spoke to the head of the Visalia Police Department Armory, who explained to her that, indeed, the SKS at issue was NOT an assault weapon and that the officer who wrote the report was wrong. The case was dismissed as to both defendants. I referred my client to a civil rights attorney and suggested that she sue the Visalia Police Department for the cost of bailing herself and her boyfriend out of jail. I don't know if they ever followed up. Had Carla and her boyfriend

---

[13] This is not a knock at Mr. P in particular, or public defenders in general. The fact is that they are overworked and doing their best.
[14] This, as the reader already knows, was factually wrong.

relied on the Public Defender's Office to protect their rights, they both would have spent somewhere between several weeks and several months in jail (and Carla would have obtained a criminal record) for something THAT WAS NEVER A CRIME.

THE MAGIC BULLETS CASE

I had a case back in 2014 that really illustrates the importance of having good expert testimony.

The defendant, let's call him Earl, had been arrested for attempted murder. Earl was a drug user. He was basically a decent kid (early 20s) but he had fallen pretty low with methamphetamine abuse. Earl wound up owing a drug dealer $20. When he didn't pay on time, the drug dealer changed it from $20 to $30, then $50, and then $80 in the span of a month. When he still didn't pay, the drug dealer started to threaten and stalk him. Eventually, fearing for his own safety, Earl's girlfriend got a gun, which she kept in their bedroom under the pillow.

One morning, things came to a head. After having been threatened over the phone and chased in a car on at least one occasion, Earl finally answered his phone at 3:00 in the morning and told the drug dealer that he had his money and that he could come to his house to get it. When the drug dealer arrived, he offered him $30 to leave him alone. The drug dealer said no and demanded $80. Earl explained that he didn't have $80, but he would get another $50 and give it to him. The drug dealer then threatened to beat the $50 out of him right then and there and said he was taking the laptop computer on the kitchen counter as collateral.

At this point Earl said that he would get additional money from the bedroom. When he came out of the bedroom, he brandished his girlfriend's firearm at the drug dealer and told him to get out. The drug dealer, in classic macho idiot drug dealer fashion, said something to the effect of "what are you going to do with that, you little pasty mother @%$#^&?" and rushed Earl to try to take his gun. Earl fired three times, striking the drug dealer twice and missing with the third round. The drug dealer (wounded but not fatally) ran through the sliding glass door (knocking it out of its frame, though amazingly not shattering it) and ran away. Earl's girlfriend, woken by the shots, called the police. The drug dealer was later found at the hospital after a Good Samaritan two blocks down called 911 on his behalf.

That is what actually happened. What the drug dealer told the police, however, was a story from another reality. The drug dealer explained that he had met Earl "hanging out on the streets." He said that he was not a drug dealer and that he had not sold any drugs to Earl, but rather that he had loaned Earl some money because he knew Earl was having financial problems and couldn't pay rent.[15] He said that he had been called to Earl's home, by Earl, and when he got there, Earl had demanded that he lend him additional money. When he refused, Earl had randomly pulled a gun on him and again demanded his wallet. When the drug dealer ran instead, he was shot in the back.

Embarrassingly, the Tulare County Sheriff's Department took this ridiculous story and arrested Earl for attempted murder. Even more embarrassingly, the Tulare County District Attorney's Office filed charges against Earl, though they agreed that he could plead guilty to assault with a firearm rather than attempted murder. Neither the Tulare County Sheriff's Department, nor the Tulare County District Attorney's Office did the least bit of ballistics work on the case. I did.

After obtaining the photographs of the scene of the "crime" as well as pictures of the "victim's" injuries, I hired a ballistics expert. Let's call him Zizi. Zizi was a retired member of the Tulare County Sheriff's Department and was embarrassed at what a slipshod job they had done in this case. He pointed out (first to me, then eventually to a jury) that one picture showed that all three shell casings were found near each other, which meant that the gun was not being moved after a moving target. He was able to map out the trajectory of each bullet to show that the first round fired went into the carpet and that the second round went straight through the drug dealer's right wrist front to back. This was consistent with the drug dealer's hand being raised, like in a grabbing motion. The third round went through the bicep and lodged into the side of the drug dealer's front ear,

---

[15] We called Earl's roommate to testify at the trial and prove that this was false.

consistent with having been fired while the drug dealer was moving towards the shooter.

Zizi destroyed the drug dealer's testimony and showed that Earl was acting in self-defense, within his own home. Earl was acquitted.

THE WORLD'S MOST WELL-ARMED CRIMINAL STREET GANG

You need to have someone interview all the supposed witnesses to make sure the police have not accidentally (or intentionally) misstated their testimony. Far too many defense attorneys simply trust what police officers put in their reports. I spent too much time around police officers as a prosecutor to make that mistake. One particular case, when I was working for the Los Angeles County District Attorney's Office, stands out. It was a gang murder case. A drive-by shooting had taken place at a house while a party was going on. One person was fatally wounded. The police, for various reasons, decided that they knew who the shooter was. Let's call him Patsy. Predictably, when questioned, two witnesses identified Patsy from a photo-lineup[16] as the shooter.

The problem came when, after the Los Angeles County District Attorney's Office filed charges against Patsy, new evidence came to light showing that he didn't do it. After the LAPD Gang Unit arrested another gang member (let's call him Pigeon), they were able to convince him to cooperate with them and tell them who the real shooter in the above case was (let's call him Shooter).

Initially it was assumed that Pigeon was lying, but the police followed up anyway. Eventually they found that Shooter drove the same type of car as identified in the shooting and possessed a gun that came back as a

---

[16] Live lineups only take place in the movies. In real criminal cases, the police will try to obtain a booking photo of their suspect. They then put that photo with five other similar looking photos taken from a booking photo database and show it to the witnesses. This is called a "photo-lineup." The most common being the "six-pack photo-lineup" where all six photographs are printed on a single page.

match to the recovered bullets. Shooter then confessed and gave specific details of the crime that only the guilty party could have known.

Young idealist that I was in those days, I wanted to believe that the two witnesses that had identified Patsy had simply made an honest mistake. The problem was that when I looked at the pictures, I realized that this was impossible. Patsy and Shooter looked NOTHING alike. The disturbing, and at the time shocking, truth was that the police had obviously coached the witnesses to pick the suspect that they "knew" was the right one. Only they were wrong. One can only imagine the number of cases where this same type of coaching has taken place and has never come to light.

I NEVER trust what the police put down in their reports to be the truth. A competent lawyer will ALWAYS have the witnesses re- interviewed by a defense investigator. In more cases than I can count, my investigators have found that when asked, witnesses admitted that the police had "suggested" to them that their picks from the photo-lineup were either right or wrong.

One investigation found that the witnesses had been shown a single photograph and asked if the person depicted committed the crime, then the next day were shown a photo-lineup with the same photograph and asked if they could pick out the person who committed the crime. In another case a witness admitted to having already seen the booking photo of the defendant used in the photo-lineup on television and in the newspapers because the police had released that photograph to the press days before the police bothered to show it to the witness.

I'm not anti-police. Readers can get a much more detailed and nuanced description of how I feel about law enforcement on my law firm's website at www.HagopianLawOffice.com. For now, it should be enough to say that I am not anti-police. I am anti-bad police. I have seen cases where the police acted in the best tradition of American heroism, and I have seen cases, like the above case, where they acted criminally and unethically. When those kinds of things happen, the police become nothing more than the world's most well-armed criminal street gang.

THE MISSING INFORMATION IN THE POLICE REPORT

If video or audiotapes exist, your attorney needs to watch or listen to them, and ideally so should you. This may seem obvious, but too many attorneys simply don't do it. Many can't or won't spend the time listening to several hours of recordings. Others try to half-ass the job by asking a secretary to listen to the tapes for them and then having the secretary tell the lawyer what the tapes said. In my opinion, this is incompetence bordering on malpractice.

Once again, we come back to the unfortunate but undeniable truth that police officers lie. Sometimes when they aren't outright lying, they are shading the truth to leave out vital information.

I had a case a few years ago where the police said that my client confessed to the crime. That's a real problem at trial. It turned out, however, that what the police report left out was the four separate times that my client asked for an attorney and said he didn't want to answer any questions. I filed a suppression motion and won a ruling that made the confession inadmissible at trial.

I read a police report a few weeks ago where the police officer stated in detail how the victims described the suspect in another attempted murder case. The police report included a detailed description of what the shooter was wearing, the type of gun they saw, and the number of shots fired. What the police report left out was one of the victims explaining that the shooter was less than 15 feet from them when he pulled the gun and that (in the words of victim/witness) *"He could have shot us easy if he had wanted to. I think he was just trying to scare us."* I suppose the police officer didn't think that observation was relevant enough for the report. Had I not listened to hours of tapes myself (or had I farmed the work out to an underling who didn't understand the legal significance of the statement) that powerful piece of defense evidence would have been missed.

Chapter 10

Legal Myths

There are a few pernicious legal myths that I run across on a semi-regular basis when talking to non-lawyers. Many of these myths have made their way into the collective consciousness through repetition in the media. Take a look. How many of these did *you* believe before you read this book?

THE LIVING WEAPON

THE MYTH — The "hands and feet" of a boxer or karate master can be considered "deadly weapons" and have to be registered. = Complete falsehood.

People v. Aguilar, 16 Cal. 4th 1023, (1997) explains that under California law a "weapon" must be something extrinsic to the body. Neither has California ever had a law requiring any type of person with any kind of special training to register themselves. Any attempt to pass a law would almost certainly fail as being too vague to implement (what kind of training makes one a "living weapon" and what doesn't?).

This myth is kept alive in part by some martial arts studios themselves who give out certificates to their students saying that they are now "lethal weapons" listed in some arcane book of international kung fu.[17] It is complete hogwash. If that list exists anywhere, it means nothing to the police or the courts.

THE FUGITIVE ESCAPE

THE MYTH—If a defendant can simply "hide out" for a few years and wait for the "statute of limitations" to run out, they can avoid ever being charged with a crime. = Almost completely false.

What is a statute of limitations?

The statute of limitations is a set of laws that say that if criminal charges are not brought within a certain number of years, they can never be brought after that. The idea of the statute of limitations is to protect individuals from having to defend themselves from wrongdoing long after any witnesses or evidence that would have helped them has vanished because of the passage of time.

How long is the statute of limitations?

In the state of California, the statute of limitations for misdemeanors is typically 1 year. For most felonies, the statute of limitations is 3 years. For certain, more serious felonies the statute of limitations is 8 years, and for murder and some sex crimes there are no statute of limitations at all.

The major flaw in this myth is that the statute of limitations does not refer to the date when the defendant *has their trial*, but the date when the prosecution *files charges*. Once the prosecution files charges against the defendant, the statute of limitations no longer applies, and the prosecution can file charges regardless of whether or not the defendant has fled the jurisdiction. In that event, an arrest warrant will be issued and the

---

[17] I know this continues because I have a niece with such a certificate. She did not take kindly to my laughing when she showed it me. I'm probably lucky that most martial arts studios teach non-violence as a virtue.

defendant will be taken into custody when they are found by law enforcement.

Why then do I say that this myth is only "almost" completely false? The reason I say this is because in a small minority of cases, a good defense attorney can get a case dismissed after the passage of several years after the prosecution has filed charges if it can be shown that law enforcement made no serious attempts to arrest the fugitive defendant. This is covered in more detail in the "Common Criminal Defense Motions" section of this book under "Serna and Doggett Motions."

THE MIRANDA DEFENSE

THE MYTH—If the police don't read a defendant his or her Miranda rights, the case needs to be dismissed. = Mostly wrong.

The case of <u>Miranda v. Arizona</u>, 384 U.S. 436 (1966) held that before the police were legally allowed to question a suspect, they needed to tell the suspect that he had a right to remain silent (and refuse to answer questions) and that the suspect had a right to a court-appointed attorney at no cost if they wanted an attorney and could not afford one.

From this, somehow, has sprung the myth that if the police do not do this, the whole case against a defendant must be dismissed as a penalty. This is wrong. What Miranda actually says is that any statement resulting from "custodial interrogation" without the subject's Miranda warnings being read must be deemed inadmissible.

If the defendant confesses during such a non-Mirandized custodial interrogation, and the confession is the only evidence that the police have, the case might be irreparably harmed when defense counsel brings a suppression motion for the Miranda violation.

In the much more likely case that Miranda warnings were not given because no interrogation was ever attempted, the lack of Miranda makes no difference, because there is no statement to suppress.

THE TRUTHFUL COP

THE MYTH — An undercover police officer must tell the truth if they are directly asked whether or not they are a cop. = Complete falsehood.

Not only are police allowed to lie to people, they are often actively encouraged to do so in their training.

In Frazier v. Cupp, 394 U.S. 731 (1969), the police lied to a murder suspect by telling him that his accomplice had already confessed.

In Oregon v. Mathiason, 429 U.S. 492 (1977), the police lied to a burglary suspect during his interrogation and told him that his fingerprints had been found at the scene.

In People v. Sims, 5 Cal. 4th 405 (1993), the police made a big show of turning off a redundant tape recorder while leaving a hidden tape recorder running to capture the defendant's confession.

In perhaps the most infamous case of all, in People v. Mays, 173 Cal App. 4th 1145 (2009), the police hooked up the suspect to a fake polygraph machine and then showed him a fake polygraph result saying that he had been lying when he denied committing a murder.

In all of these cases, the first three of which are United States Supreme Court cases, it was held that the police were allowed to use lies and deception in their investigations and interrogations.

In the face of just how much police lie on a daily basis, the myth that an undercover officer would have to come clean if asked about their "being a cop" is truly laughable.

THE RABID BULLDOG

Clients are often surprised by the fact that defense attorneys and prosecuting attorneys, or even defense attorneys and judges, don't show constant and obvious signs of hating each other. It can be disturbing to those clients to see their lawyer having a friendly conversation, even joking and laughing with a prosecutor who they think of as "THE ENEMY."

The Myth—You want to find yourself the biggest, meanest, ugliest, most obnoxious defense attorney possible, because that person will fight the hardest and get you the best results.

Loud, mean, and generally unlikable defense attorneys do certainly exist, but this is a professional flaw, not an asset. Larry H. Parker has cursed the legal professional with the public image that their counsel should act like a MMA fighter with a chip on their shoulder. Larry Parker used to run television commercials[18] where he put on his angry face and said things like "I'll fight for you!" (a phrase which is now almost a requirement of all lawyer advertising.) But "fighting" for a client in the courtroom bears pretty much zero relationship to street-fighting in the parking lot.

Throwing mean looks and insults, let alone punches, wouldn't help my clients. What does help my clients is having a good professional working relationship with the judges and prosecutors who have the power to give my clients what they want *without unnecessary fighting*.

That doesn't mean that I'm a pushover . . . far from it. If the only way to get what the client wants is to call witnesses, file legal briefs, and explain to the judge how the prosecutor is an unreasonable idiot, that is exactly what I will do. That is exactly what any good defense attorney will do. If the judges themselves get the law wrong, we will call them out on it, and if explaining their error doesn't make them change their ruling, we will file an appeal to a higher court and embarrass them in public for their mistakes. Once again, that is what any good lawyer would do. The difference here between the real "fighting" for a client that I do and the fiction of the "rabid dog" lawyer that too many have in their head is that I don't go out of my way to be confrontational and obnoxious when it won't help.

---

[18] Most memorable for showing a paraplegic man from the neck up shouting the line "Larry Parker got me two-point-one million!"

I cannot stress this point enough: a courtroom is a not a place for brawling. It is a place for sophisticated argument according to a set of mind-boggling, complex rules. This is a game for educated and refined intellect, not knuckle-dragging aggression. If I hear a lawyer raise their voice and see them looking angry or offended in the courtroom, I know this a bad lawyer. If I see it in my opposing counsel, I know my client is going to have a good day.

THE CHARGE-DROPPING VICTIM

The Myth — The victim of a crime must agree to bring charges, and those charges can be dropped by the victim if they change their mind. = False.

There was a time, many years ago, when the criminal courts did work this way. The victim literally brought charges against the defendant and the prosecutor sought to prove those charges in court.

This is no longer the case. Today, the decision whether to bring or drop charges rests entirely with the prosecuting agency (usually the district or city attorney's office). The idea behind the change in the way cases are brought and controlled goes to the philosophical question of who is the wronged party when a crime takes place. Years ago, we said that only the victim was the wronged party, and so only the victim's opinion about whether to proceed with a case mattered. More recently our philosophy has changed to consider that when a person breaks a law, any law, that it is *all* of the people within the society the defendant lives in who are injured by that breach of order. It is therefore the representative of the people (the prosecutor) who decides how to prosecute the case.

While the prosecutor in any given case would certainly be wise to take the position of the victim into account (and in many cases the prosecution simply cannot win without the cooperation of the victim) the victim cannot make the prosecutor drop a case.

THE CASTLE-STANDING GROUND

The Myth — You can shoot anyone who breaks into your house, and if you happen to shoot them outside, you should drag the body inside. = Mostly false.

Strictly speaking, where a person is shot has no legal significance at all. The question in such a shooting is whether or not self-defense applies. The law of self defense says that a person is only allowed to use the minimum force that will safely prevent another person from committing a crime against them and may only use lethal force to prevent great bodily injury or death from being inflicted on someone.

Therefore, if an obviously unarmed midget breaks into the home of a completely healthy bodybuilder, he will not be allowed to shoot them and then claim self-defense. Equally true is that if a person runs up and steals a purse and runs away, they cannot be shot in the back to recover the stolen property.

The reason that I say that this myth is only "mostly" false is that in the vast majority of cases where someone shoots an intruder in their home, the requirements for self-defense will have been met. The reason for this is that the individual whose home is broken into does not need to take any unnecessary risk to determine the threat posed by the perpetrator who is breaking in. Therefore, if someone breaks into your home, at night in the dark, it is completely reasonable to assume that they are armed with a firearm and they intend to kill you in order to rob you. Given that most home invasions take place at night in the dark, you really *can* shoot just about anyone who breaks into your home and use self-defense as an excuse. This is not because the house has special rules, but because the always-present laws of self-defense work out this way in most home invasions.

As for shooting the body and dragging it into the house, your greatest problem would be the obvious trail of blood that it would leave. As someone who has seen a great many pictures of a great many shooting scenes, I can tell you, people who are shot bleed A LOT.

THE DUMP TRUCK

The Myth—Any lawyer who settles a case rather than going to trial is lazy and not looking out for their clients' best interest.[19] = Mostly false.

Television has taught many people that good lawyers go to trial on behalf of their clients. From this, many people have inferred that if a lawyer seeks to settle a case rather than argue in front of a jury, something must be wrong with that lawyer. Both the premise and the conclusion above are wrong.

The truth is that settlement is the right option in the majority of cases. I would go so far as to say that a lawyer who advises their client to go to trial in most cases would be so incompetent as to be guilty of malpractice. The reason for this is simple: most people charged with crimes are guilty, and there is a mountain of evidence proving that they are guilty. If you are charged with a crime and are NOT guilty, congratulations, you are in the minority. It is for your benefit that we have this whole system of criminal justice set up! You should probably go to trial. For the rest of defendants, however, there are a few very good reasons why a criminal defense lawyer might suggest their client accept a plea bargain.

1. A judge will almost always offer to give a defendant a break if they plead guilty rather than go to trial. The fact is that if every defendant who was accused of a crime went to trial, the criminal courts would come to a standstill. We simply do not have enough courts or judges, or even enough prosecutors, to allow all of those trials to go on. For this reason, judges give defendants a break in their sentence when they plead guilty rather than take their case in front of a jury.

    Does the fact that a defendant may eventually take a plea bargain mean that his or her lawyer is not important? No, it does not. That,

---

[19] The term "dump truck lawyer" (mostly applied to public defender lawyers) is a reference to those attorneys who "dump" all of their clients on the first day by telling everyone that they need to settle their cases immediately. This results in the lawyer being able to do little to no work and their clients getting a bad deal at best and pleading out to false charges at worst.

too, is a myth perpetrated by people who know just enough to sound educated (see "the jailhouse lawyer" below) but not enough to actually understand what is going on.

The reason that your lawyer is important, even if you eventually take a plea bargain, is the obvious fact that not all plea bargains are equally good.

Your lawyer may be able to get a particularly good deal if they can convince the prosecution that there is any chance of a not-guilty verdict. Prosecutors hate to lose. They are expected to win every one of their cases, and if they do not, it can negatively affect their career prospects. For this reason, a lawyer who can convince them that there is a substantial likelihood that the defendant will be found not guilty will often be able to negotiate a good plea bargain sentence that will be much less than what the defendant would have received if they went to trial and were convicted.

NOTE: A "substantial likelihood" does not mean more likely than not. It can still be more likely than not that a defendant will be convicted (say a 75% chance) and the prosecutor will want to make a deal to eliminate the 25% chance that they will lose.

Having a lawyer who has a reputation for going to trial and winning and for not accepting "bad deals" from prosecutors really, REALLY helps in these negotiations. One of the major weaknesses in having a public defender represent you is that very few public defenders have this kind of reputation.

2. A sentence after trial will almost always result in jail time, but oftentimes what the government wants is something other than jail time. In many cases, a good lawyer can craft a good "sentence" that

---

[20] And to be fair, there are some prosecutors who are pragmatists and figure that a sure thing of getting a lesser than deserved punishment for a guilty defendant is better than risking that the defendant will not be punished at all after trial.

doesn't involve their client ever setting foot inside a jail cell. [21] Here is a small list of things that the government may want that do not involve jail time.

- The defendant will attend counseling for drug or alcohol addiction.
- This may mean attending group and or individual therapy or, in more extreme cases, going into an inpatient treatment program.
- The defendant will wear an alcohol monitor.
- The defendant will attend anger management.
- The defendant will attend parenting classes.
- The defendant will pay for all the damages they caused.
- The defendant will get their suspended license unsuspended.
- The defendant will complete community service.
- The defendant will attend a specialized "court" program such as a Drug Court, Veterans Court, or Mental Health Court.
- OTHER. The range of sentence crafting is limited only by your lawyer's imagination.

I represented a 23-year-old client accused of the statutory rape of a 17-year-old victim. As part of his "plea bargain," he agreed to marry the pregnant victim and take care of her and their child for at least the 5-year term of felony probation.

I represented another young man a few years ago who was charged with possession of child pornography. We were able to keep this young man out of jail in large part because we enrolled him in a program for people with pornography addiction, AND we made it a term of his probation that his father (a former federal law enforcement officer) would be given complete access to his Internet history on both his home computer and cell phone through a program called "covenant eyes."

---

[21] Or at least a plea bargain that involves them spending the least amount of time necessary in that jail cell.

I represented a third young man recently, who was coming into court on his third car theft charge. Because I was able to explain his situation to the judge, including his history of drug use and lack of education or work experience, I was able to convince the judge to have this young man enter a program called Delancy Street, which is a live-in jobs training program for ex-cons.

In the above case, we gave the client what he wanted (a way out of prison), and we gave the state what they wanted (a way to end this person's cycle of crime and arrest and thus make the streets safer). Everybody wins.

Why then do I say that this myth is only "mostly false?" The reason I say this is because "dump truck" lawyers DO exist. They exist both in the Public Defender's Office and, even more disturbingly, in the private sector.

In the private sector, there are certain law firms that have made being dump truck lawyers their business model. These firms spend an insane amount on advertising (and will, as a result, usually be the first firm listed on Google, be the first postcard you receive after an arrest, and have the most and shiniest billboards in your city). They undercut the entire lawyer market on price (charging as little as half of what competent lawyers will charge for the same representations), then they send baby lawyers a few days out of law school to plead out all of their clients on the first day.

Decent, competent lawyers refer to these types of firms as "lawyer mills." They simply churn out guilty pleas and rely on the fact that because criminal defense has so few repeat customers, the fact that they are terrible at their job won't hurt them. They are able to charge less than their competition because they never intend for a lawyer who knows anything to spend any time working on their clients' cases. Beware the lawyer mill. You would be better off with the Public Defender's Office.

THE LAST-MINUTE DEAL

The Myth — Prosecutors wait till just before the trial starts to make their best plea bargain deal to the defendants. = Almost always false.

This is one of those myths that persists among "jailhouse lawyers" (inmates who didn't know enough to keep themselves out of custody but feel the need to tell everyone else how they should ignore their real-life lawyers and litigate their case). The reasoning, at a very short first glance, seems sound. Prosecutors don't want to do trials, but they want the defendant to get the most time in prison possible. The prosecutor therefore will make bad offers, hoping to dupe the scared defendants into taking early pleas, and will reserve their "best" offers for those brave enough to stick it out until almost the end.

Now that sounds good, if you know absolutely nothing about the law. Here are all the facts that this line of "reasoning" ignores:

1. Every day the prosecutor works on a case, he or she has that much less incentive to settle, because there is that much less work to do in total. On the eve of trial, the prosecutor has done SO MUCH work on a case that they probably WANT the trial to happen.
2. Most cases are slam dunk winners for most prosecutors and most (though not all) prosecutors are not afraid of losing when they have a mountain of evidence on their side. Lawyers who know those prosecutors' individual personalities are best able to tell you how to negotiate with them. This isn't a "one size fits all" kind of a thing.
3. The prosecutor is not the only person affecting the sentence a defendant is given. The judge also has a hand in deciding the sentence, and judges go out of their way (in order to clear their own desks over the long run) to make it known that they are most lenient to those defendants who settle their cases early.

Why do I say that this is only "almost" always false? Because there is the rare case where the last offer really will be the best one. This may happen when:

1. The prosecutor changes for some reason.
2. The defense is only able, on the eve of trial, to obtain and to show the prosecutor great exculpatory evidence that may prevent a conviction.

3. Law enforcement themselves come up with exculpatory evidence at the last minute (this is all but unheard of, but I have seen it in two out of literally hundreds of cases).
4. The prosecution's witnesses don't show up for trial.

I myself have cases where I plan on settling at the last minute. In almost all of these cases, it is because I feel that the prosecution will have problems getting their witnesses to the court for trial. When this happens, I almost always move the case to trial as quickly as possible by refusing to "waive time" and demanding a trial within the statutory limits by such demands. Again, this is not a one size fits all thing.

THE OLD, WISE MILLIONARE SUPERLAWYER

The Myth—The most experienced and/or most expensive lawyer will get the defendant the best results. = False.

You probably don't want a lawyer who lives out of his car, and you certainly don't want a lawyer who is just out of law school, but the idea that increasing wealth and experience always indicate increasing competence is a mistaken one.

As in all professions, the law has quite a few practitioners (I know several) who have decades of experience doing their job . . . badly.

There are also quite a few lawyers, with fancy offices, who wear thousand-dollar suits and carry designer briefcases or purses . . . who I would not trust to get my dog out of the pound, let alone a friend out of jail.

You may ask . . . how can this be? How can a bad attorney be successful? Many of them aren't. There are a number of lawyers who have inherited their wealth (and some of them their firms and offices) from their parents. They are mediocre lawyers who enjoy the trappings of other people's success. Some other bad lawyers ARE themselves successful because (both fortunately and unfortunately) criminal defense is a field with very few repeat customers.

You also can't tell a "good" lawyer from a "bad" lawyer by their "win/loss" record, because no such thing really exists in the real world. In the real world of criminal justice, the vast majority of cases are not clear wins or losses. A case that settles may be considered a win or a loss depending on the strength of the evidence. Likewise, a conviction for disturbing the peace (an infraction) when a person is charged with murder
at the outset of the case is certainly a win for the defendant but may well be claimed as a win for the prosecution.[22]

The news isn't all bad. There are a few legal myths, the truth of which very much favors those accused of crimes:

DNA CASES, FINGERPRINT CASES, GUN SHOT RESIDUE CASES, ETC. ARE UNBEATABLE

Not true. The popular television series CSI has convinced many people around the world that crime scene investigators are able to perform magic in the laboratory and that the tests they perform are able to 100% solve cases, no questions, end of story. The truth is much more complicated.

Take DNA evidence for example. DNA is the "gold standard" of evidence, but it isn't unchallengeable. A friend and colleague of mine earned a not-guilty plea recently on a child molestation case. The prosecutor was shocked by the loss. Shocked and appalled. They had been certain that once their CSI guy came in and showed that the defendant's DNA was on his stepdaughter's underwear that a conviction would be easy. It wasn't. My friend retained the services of a DNA expert witness, who re-examined the evidence. The first thing that he found was that the DNA found was based on minute trace amounts on the fabric. The source of the DNA also was not semen, as the CSI report had wrongly assumed

---

[22] Many district attorney's offices use this fact to outright lie about their success rate, claiming "We convict 97% of the people we charge!" when in fact a far greater than 3% of those cases were settled for, or went to trial and were convicted of, far lesser charges that were brought by the prosecuting agency. I could easily claim a 99.99% success rate for my clients if I considered it a "win" every time the client got anything but the maximum sentence for the crime they were initially charged with. These "win/loss" numbers have no meaning.

(their lab guy had failed to perform competent checks), but skin cells. The expert was able to testify in court that when laundry for multiple people was done in the same household (as was the case here) that skin cells not only can, but almost invariably will travel between pieces of cloth.

There were also other inconsistencies with the evidence. The victim had claimed acts, not necessary to describe here, which would have left evidence that was not present. The lead investigator on the case uncovered both that this girl had a good friend who had made similar (unfounded) molestation allegations against a teacher and that the "victim" in this case was motivated by a desire for her mother and her birth father to get back together (her mother had left the birth father for the client). The police had simply failed to do their homework because they thought the DNA evidence "magic bullet" was unchallengeable. It isn't. There are other cases I am aware of where the same lab contaminated their two samples with each other and then (of course) they matched. The lab technician simply bungled the test.

Similar things can be said of fingerprints and ballistics and any other kind of scientific evidence. A good lawyer always knows a good expert who can test the government's evidence to see what they did wrong.

DUI CASES ARE UNBEATABLE IF THE LAB RESULTS SHOW INTOXICATION

Not true. As I sit here writing this, I can recall two cases, one with a blood test result of .24 (three times the legal limit) and another with a blood test result of .15 where the defendant walked away without being convicted of anything. In the first case, the whole matter was thrown out because the police lacked probable cause to make the stop, and we won our suppression motion. In the second case, we earned an acquittal in front of a jury because while the defendant was indeed drunk, he was not the person driving the car. That person had fled the scene and while he refused to admit it at trial, he came off (after a bit of brilliant cross examination) as such a dirt bag on the witness stand, that the jury was ready to convict *him* after they acquitted my client.

Final Thoughts on Politics, Underfunding, and Cynicism

I have three last words on things I have learned both as a deputy district attorney and in several years since as a criminal defense attorney: Politics, Underfunding, and Cynicism.

The criminal courts are political. Crime is political. The so-called "justice system" is political. The district attorney, whom all of the other prosecutors work for and under, is elected to office and must run periodically for re-election. Judges also, while mostly appointed (at least initially) by the governor, can be challenged in popular elections. The result of these politics is a criminal court system as much (or more) interested in putting on a good show for reporters as it is in doing actual justice. Judges lose elections when they can be painted as "soft on crime." District attorneys win re-elections when they can point to their stellar win- loss record and point out all of the "bad guys" they have put away behind bars.

The criminal courts are also underfunded. The California Superior Court System (the supermajority of which is made up of the criminal court system) is so underfunded that a few short years ago, the clerk's offices had to scale back their operating hours, and for a short time, courthouses were dark one day per month in order to save money. While we are no longer in quite that desperate a situation, the court system is still underfunded, as is evidenced by our crumbling courtrooms and courthouses.

These two things, politics and underfunding, have combined to create the plea bargain criminal court system that we now have. As stated earlier, judges and prosecutors are forced to settle most of their cases, because if even half of the defendants who appeared demanded a trial, the entire system would grind to a halt. Neither the judge nor the prosecutor really has much time to think about your case. They run "justice mills" and need to keep moving lest they get behind on their paperwork. Herein comes the final word: Cynicism.

There are of course exceptions, but by and large most prosecutors and judges are cynics. They assume that you are guilty and they don't want to hear your denials. It is understandable how such cynicism comes to be; indeed, most people accused of crimes ARE guilty. Years and years of guilty people coming before them and lying to them simply wears down the capacity of most prosecutors and judges to give a fair hearing to your claim of innocence. They don't want to hear it. They will if they are forced to. But, they WILL need to be forced.

Into this quasi-political, underfunded, hyper-technical, rule-based system comes *you*, the criminal defendant. I hope that this book has helped to answer some of your more basic questions about what has, will, and might happen to you. I leave you, however, with this caution: this book, indeed a whole room of books, will not prepare you to deal with the criminal justice system alone. Hopefully you are now in a better position to assist your attorney, but you will need an attorney. Choose a guide through this maze, and choose carefully. Your life, as you know it, may literally depend on it.

Notes to Discuss with Your Attorney

Use this section to make notes about what you need to discuss with your attorney and what questions you need to ask.

_____

_____

_____

_____

_____

_____

_____

_____

_____

Greg Hagopian

www.ingramcontent.com/pod-product-compliance
Lightning Source LLC
Chambersburg PA
CBHW050553210326
41521CB00008B/948